FROM TAKEOFF TO LANDING

Everything You Wanted to Know About Airplanes But Had No One to Ask

Including:
- Why doors *can't* open accidentally in flight
- Bumps, thumps and turbulence—what's normal, what's not
- How planes actually fly

And much more!

Ed Sternstein and Todd Gold

ISBN 0-671-72217-4

Discover the Reassuring Facts about Flying

Q. What happens if the plane gets a flat tire?
A. Nothing. The remaining tires are enough to support the plane.

Q. On a long flight will I be breathing stale air?
A. No. New air enters the plane at nearly 6000 cubic feet per minute, enough to completely recycle the air every 180 seconds.

Q. Could someone accidentally—or intentionally—open a door in mid-flight?
A. No. When the plane is pressurized the interior pressure locks the doors in place, making them impossible to open.

Q. What if my seat has a defective oxygen mask?
A. Four oxygen masks are available for every three seats and are deployed automatically as needed—or manually at any time.

Q. Will the plane fall if the engines fail?
A. No. The pilot will lower the plane's nose and glide. In fact, on almost every flight there comes a point during the descent when the pilots will pull the power back to idle and let the plane glide. Gliding is a normal part of almost every flight.

From Takeoff to Landing will tell you everything about a commercial plane ride, from what the ground crew is doing before the flight to why pilots sometimes choose to make a "firm arrival" rather than a "grease job" touchdown. Turn the page, and rediscover the magic of flying.

FROM
TAKEOFF
═══ TO ═══
LANDING

*Everything You Wanted to Know
About Airplanes
But Had No One to Ask*

ED STERNSTEIN
TODD GOLD

POCKET BOOKS
New York   London   Toronto   Sydney   Tokyo   Singapore

An *Original* Publication of POCKET BOOKS

POCKET BOOKS, a division of Simon & Schuster Inc.
1230 Avenue of the Americas, New York, NY 10020

Sternstein, Ed.
     From takeoff to landing: everything you wanted to know about
airplanes but had no one to ask / Ed Sternstein, Todd Gold.
          p.   cm.
     ISBN 0-671-72217-4 : $7.95
     1. Aeronautics, Commercial.   2. Air travel.   I. Gold, Todd.
II. Title.
TL552.S74 1991
629.133' 340423—dc20   91-9306
                                                         CIP

First Pocket Books trade paperback printing July 1991

10 9 8 7 6 5 4 3 2 1

To my bride, Alexandra,
and our children Kate and Scott

—E.S.

To Abby and Eliza

—T.G.

ACKNOWLEDGMENTS

I wish I could list the names of the thousands of airline employees who make my job as a pilot so rewarding and safe. It is a pleasure to work with all of you.

Thanks to Captain Stefan Meyer, a real captain's captain. His skills and leadership provide inspiration for all of us.

Thanks to Dr. David Stone and his wife Kimberly, whose fascination with flying was the motivation for this book.

Thanks to Captain John Moran, my liaison with Delta Air Lines. From the beginning of this project he offered me support and guidance.

A special thanks to my parents, Dr. Martin Sternstein and Phyllis Lavitt, who always encouraged me to pursue my dreams.

Thanks to Jane Chelius and Dana Isaacson, our editors at Pocket Books, for their professionalism and editorial skills.

And I especially want to thank my family—Alexandra, Kate, and Scott—for their patience and understanding through the long process of writing this book.

Thank you all.

—E.S.

Thank you to:

My parents, Rita Gold and Martin Gold; my grandparents, Dave and Eleanor Gold; my grandmother, Nellie Klein, who traveled by train . . . until recently; my in-laws, Arthur and Eileen Schwartz; and my fellow white-knuckler, my sister Kimberly.

Also: Dan Strone, a literary pilot; Lisa Millman—don't be scared—er, too scared; Jainah Hamann, my all-time

ACKNOWLEDGMENTS

favorite flight attendant; and Motley Crüe, whose tour plane was a real Dr. Feelgood.

Then there are: all the airline pilots I've ever had who've announced that the bumps are nothing to worry about; my daughters, Abby and Eliza; and my wife Beth.

—T.G.

CONTENTS

Introduction   1

Part I: The Aircraft

Chapter 1
PREFLIGHT PLANNING   7

Chapter 2
THE FLIGHT CREW   15

Chapter 3
THE AIRCRAFT: EXTERIOR AND SAFETY   23

Chapter 4
THE AIRCRAFT: INTERIOR AND SAFETY   39

Chapter 5
COCKPIT PREPARATION AND AIRCRAFT SYSTEMS   51

Chapter 6
BASIC AERODYNAMICS   71

Chapter 7
EMERGENCY WARNING SYSTEMS   81

Chapter 8
MAINTENANCE   93

CONTENTS

Part II: The Flight

Chapter 9
PUSHBACK, ENGINE START, AND TAXI   101

Chapter 10
TAKEOFF AND DEPARTURE   119

Chapter 11
CLIMB, CRUISE, AND DESCENT   131

Chapter 12
WEATHER PHENOMENA   147

Chapter 13
APPROACH TO LAND   155

Chapter 14
LANDING AND TAXI IN   171

Afterword   183

Aviation Abbreviations   185

Glossary   189

INTRODUCTION

Most of us were introduced to the marvels of air travel in the same way. It started with a strange noise, a curious roar of combustion high up in the air, and the wonderful sight of an enormous birdlike contraption streaking gracefully through the sky.

"What is that?" we asked our parents, wide-eyed and fascinated.

"An airplane," they answered. "Can you say 'airplane'?"

From then on, we continued to point at airplanes flying overhead. We pretended to fly by extending our arms and imitating the whooshing sound of powerful engines. If we were lucky, we caught sight of a streaking plane leaving long, white, billowy jet trails in the blue sky, like some kind of heavenly handwriting.

At some point we got on a plane and discovered the magic of flying for ourselves.

Impressions of flight are formed early. However, those impressions change over time, influenced by newspapers, tales from friends and family, television, movies, and finally, by personal experience.

For many fliers an airplane trip is one of life's most fascinating and wondrous experiences. One minute you're on the ground, the next you're soaring through the air on a technological magic carpet ride. Consider this:

The Wright brothers' entire first flight could have taken place inside the fuselage of one of today's jumbo jets. The engine of a modern widebody is larger in diameter than an old DC-3 airplane. Most commercial aircraft are able to fly at an altitude of more than eight miles and at speeds of nearly ten miles per minute. And when it comes to landing, state-of-the-art navigational equipment can pinpoint a precise spot clear on the other side of the globe.

For some of us, as we grow older and more cynical, an airplane flight becomes cause for concern and worry. After we buckle ourselves in, our minds whirl with myriad questions. What would happen if the plane lost an engine? What if it lost two engines? Or what if all the engines stopped in mid-flight?

What if one of the hydraulic systems failed? The electrical system? What if the cabin lost pressure? What about thunderstorms, lightning and hail? What is turbulence? Can it damage the plane? What are those strange noises?

Other people are even worse fliers. They don't want the first thing to do with airplanes. These are the downright fearful passengers who fly only out of necessity—and not without a drink, a tranquilizer, or a comforting hand to hold. Yet time and time again, statistics confirm the relative safety of air travel. There are over 17,000 domestic flights 365 days a year, with nary a single minor incident.

But numbers provide little comfort to the white-knuckle flier. Why? Simply because statistics don't address the overwhelming fear of not being in control, of the unknown.

Then, there are those most laid-back of air travelers, the nonchalant fliers. These are people for whom airplanes are merely transportation, a convenient and quick way to get from point A to point B. The nonchalant flier is primarily concerned with good service, timeliness, and a hassle-free trip. If they have any thoughts about air travel, they revolve around mechanical problems that cause delays, gate-holds, runway traffic, and order of takeoff.

To varying degrees most air travelers, whether frequent or otherwise, fall into all of these categories—a little concerned, a little fearful, admittedly fascinated, and, at times, nonchalant. How these emotions are balanced depends in large part on how much we know about airplanes. Unfortunately, routine information about air travel—the nuts and bolts of how airplanes work—has not been readily available to those with nontechnical backgrounds.

Even though more than sixty million Americans fly routinely every year—more if international flights are considered—passengers have very little knowledge of how airplanes fly and what pilots do. Most passengers don't even understand basic aerodynamics. Often, one's fear of flying is in inverse proportion to one's knowledge of flight. Were people to know more, they would be less afraid.

That's the reason for this book, *From Takeoff to Landing.* It will attempt to demystify the secrets of flying. The questions every curious airline passenger has wanted to know but had no one to ask will be addressed in nontechnical, easy-to-understand language.

The fascinated flier will find discussions of all the buttons and gauges in the cockpit. The nervous traveler will discover the meaning of all those strange noises and sounds that seem to crop up during flight, as well as what's actually happening when the ride gets bumpy. Even catastrophic "what if" situations will be discussed, as will flight crew training and certification.

By the end, you might feel as if you could fly the plane—even if you're sitting in coach!

There is a reason this book is more comprehensive than any previous books on commercial air travel. Ed Sternstein has been flying for twenty-one years, the last twelve as a pilot with Delta Air Lines. In that time, he has experienced the gamut of flight conditions, from turbulence to hazardous weather to mechanical malfunctions to various system anomalies. Yet all of his flights, regardless of the problem or discrepancy that popped up, have been completely safe.

How can this be so? Because of the comprehensive system of checks and balances between the pilots, flight attendants, mechanics, dispatchers, fuelers, air traffic controllers, the FAA, and everyone else involved in the flight of a commercial airline—all the things most air travelers don't know about but should in order to feel safe and secure.

The book works, too. Todd Gold, Ed's co-author, is a journalist and frequent flier who estimates he has flown at least once a month for the past eight years and never enjoyed a single flight. In turbulence, he has been known to pick up the in-flight telephone and dial 911. Working with Ed has changed his mind about flying.

"I worked on this book out of absolute necessity," he says. "I've been told numerous times that there is only one way to overcome a fear of flying, and that's to learn to fly.

"This book won't actually teach you how to fly a 747, but it's the first book I have ever encountered—and I've read them all—that comes close. Read it, and you'll know almost everything about a commercial plane ride, from what the ground crew is doing before the flight to why the pilot turns on the seat-belt sign when it gets rocky."

Adds Ed, "To be honest, I'm more comfortable traveling as a pilot than a passenger. I like to fly and I like to be in control.

"But when I am a passenger, which is frequent, I enjoy answering questions about aviation and explaining the various sounds and sensations of flying. And when I tell people that the odd noises, turbulence, in-air vibrations, and less-than-perfect landings are routine, it's because I understand what's going on.

"Now it's your turn to understand. It's your turn to know the pilot's perspective. It's your turn to have the information that helps make flying both fascinating and fun."

PART

I

The Aircraft

CHAPTER 1

PREFLIGHT PLANNING

PLANNING THE ROUTE, ALTITUDE, AND SPEED

An airline is a highly technical labor-intensive, service-oriented business. More than 100 person-hours are spent preparing for every one hour a pilot spends flying.

A major airline employs approximately 60,000 people. Of those, 12 percent (or 7500) are pilots; 22 percent (or more than 13,000) are flight attendants; and 7 percent (5500) are mechanics.

The other 34,000 employees are equally as vital, but are not always given equal credit. The reservations staff, marketing personnel, passenger service agents, crew schedulers, dispatchers, central load planners, cargo and baggage handlers, fuel servicemen, cabin service, training instructors, lawyers, secretaries, etc. are all an integral part of a safe and reliable airline. In fact it takes more than 150 employees to operate just one aircraft. The larger airlines operate more than 400 aircraft.

A major U.S. domestic airline will schedule roughly 2500 flights daily, departing around the clock every day of the year. It doesn't sound all that impressive until you realize that works out to nearly one departure every thirty seconds.

Equally impressive is that, even when you take into account weather and mechanical cancellations, the airline completes nearly 98 percent of its published flight schedule.

WHERE DOES YOUR FLIGHT BEGIN?

Two hours before each and every flight at one central location—usually near the corporate headquarters—the dispatch department begins planning your flight. One hundred dispatchers, who, like pilots and mechanics, are licensed by the Federal Aviation Administration (FAA) are responsible for the preliminary planning of your flight. This includes the route, cruise altitude, fuel load, and coordinating your flight plan with Air Traffic Control (ATC).

CHECKING THE WEATHER

The dispatcher's first step is to check the weather. They review and compare reports from both the airline's own meteorological department and the U.S. National Weather Service, which monitors weather at over 600 locations in the domestic U.S.

The dispatcher looks for forecasts of hazardous or severe in-flight weather that must be avoided, including thunderstorms, squall lines (groups of thunderstorms), hail, tornadoes, hurricanes, severe ice, windshear, and moderate to severe turbulence.

In pilot parlance, forecasts of severe weather are called SIGMETS. The National Weather Service issues SIGMETS and transmits these forecasts to the airline's meteorological and dispatch department—as well as to pilots in-flight—as they become available.

After checking for possible extreme weather, the dispatchers compare the en route forecast with the actual weather received from satellite photos, radar images, and actual pilot reports (called PIREPS). Among pilots, PIREPS are the next best thing to being there.

In the absence of hazardous weather, additional attention is given to the forecasted en route winds, including the location and intensity of the *jet stream*. The jet stream is wind of 75 knots (86 mph) or greater, spanning a distance of 300 miles or more. Occasionally it can get up to 200 knots (230 mph). (To convert knots into miles per hour, multiply the figure by 1.15.)

As a tailwind, the jet stream can shorten en route time considerably. In most cases, when it is turbulence free, it is a time- and fuel-saving asset. As a headwind, the opposite is true.

The dispatcher will next have the meteorological department locate the *tropopause:* the layer of atmosphere separating the troposphere (the layer located nearest the earth's surface) and the stratosphere, the uppermost atmosphere. In the winter it begins in the mid-30,000 foot level, and in the summer it's located in the 50,000 foot range.

Above the tropopause the temperature is fairly constant at approximately −56 degrees. Since temperature changes are the main ingredient for the formation of all weather, it follows that above the troposphere there is basically no weather.

The surface weather and forecasts at both the departure and destination airports will be reviewed next. The dispatcher's surface weather analysis will also include any airport alerts—such as construction or ongoing maintenance that would alter the useful length of the runway— and field condition reports, which would include such things as standing snow or ice.

SELECTING A ROUTE

The next step: How is the plane going to fly from point A to point B?

The criteria is safety first, passenger comfort second, and

cost third. The adage within the industry is "Maximum safety at minimum cost."

Because the first rule in picking a route is safety, weather is always a primary consideration.

However, the second consideration in selecting a route is working within the Air Traffic Control (ATC) system. For both takeoff and arrival there are ATC predetermined routes called SIDS—Standard Instrument Departures— and STARS—Standard Terminal Arrival Routes. Think of them as freeway on-and-off ramps in the sky. These published routes are depicted on navigational charts carried by all airline pilots.

When planes depart an airport, they follow SIDS. There may be as many as eight to ten SIDS per airport, depending on the size of the airport. All planes flying to their destinations on the same *general* compass heading—no matter how close or far their destinations may be—will be on the same SID. Aircraft with destinations in a different general direction will be on another published SID. These departure corridors end at particular points, where planes then join en route airways (highways in the sky).

Those arriving at airports are following STARS. These arrival routes sometimes begin more than 200 miles away from the airport. At this point Air Traffic Control begins lining up the aircraft on these off-ramps in the sky and sequencing them for landing. Some STARS allow for long, gradual descents at the discretion of the pilots. Other STARS, particularly if there is more than one major airport in close proximity, dictate specific speeds and crossing altitudes (exact altitudes at exact locations). Usually the time you reach the arrival gate for the STAR is also the time the flight attendants need to prepare the cabin for arrival. The seat-belt sign is turned on at this time.

PICKING AN ALTITUDE

The first two considerations in selecting an altitude are weather and winds, which have already been discussed. The third criteria is the performance of the aircraft.

Each plane has a maximum altitude it can fly. For instance, a Boeing 767 can cruise up to 43,000 feet. However, when the plane's weight is taken into account, the optimum altitude for fuel economy may not equal the maximum altitude. The goal is to fly as close to the optimum altitude as possible.

The fourth and sometimes the overriding component in picking a cruising altitude is the ATC-mandated *separation between aircraft.*

When flying on an easterly heading—0 to 179 degrees—planes cruise at odd-numbered altitudes: 23,000; 25,000; 27,000; and 29,000 feet. When flying in a westerly direction —180 to 359 degrees—planes fly at even altitudes: 24,000; 26,000; and 28,000.

Above 29,000 feet, aircraft are required to maintain a 2000-foot vertical separation.

To maintain altitude separation between aircraft flying in opposite directions, the easterly heading "odd" altitudes are defined as 33,000, 37,000, 41,000, and 45,000, feet. The westerly heading "even altitudes are defined as 31,000, 35,000, 39,000, and 43,000 feet. If your optimum altitude is other than a cardinal altitude, the safety of aircraft separation takes precedence over aircraft economy.

PICKING A CRUISE SPEED

The consideration is minimum cost at a minimum time.

Optimum cruising speeds average 460 knots, which is 540 mph. This works out to about nine miles per minute. A proposed cruise speed is filed with ATC before the flight, and a deviation of plus or minus 10 knots must be reported. Why? Because many planes are flying the same routes, and any change will effect the departure and arrival gates as well as the separation between airplanes on similar routes.

Maximum speeds are higher than 460 knots, closer to 500 knots (or almost 600 mph). But as little as a 4-knot variation from optimum cruise speed will increase the fuel flow from one to two percent, which increases the fuel cost. Since the cost of fuel makes up nearly 45 percent of the per hour cost of an airplane and 20 to 25 percent of the total operations expense, flying faster or slower can be expensive.

SELECTING A FUEL LOAD

The two factors absolutely critical in aviation are fuel and weather. They are monitored continuously.

The fuel load is determined in a straightforward manner. First, trip fuel—the amount needed to get the plane from departure to its scheduled destination. By law, trip fuel takes into account numerous variables, including increased flight times due to forecasted headwinds, weather that must be circumnavigated, the actual route—not always the shortest distance between two points—and any anticipated delays.

Second, enough fuel is planned in case it becomes necessary to take an alternative route. This takes into account bad weather. If the weather at the flight's destination is forecasted to be less than a 2000-foot cloud cover *and* less than three miles visibility, then there must be enough fuel to fly to the most distant alternate.

Third, the plane must have "hold fuel" for unforecast delays. Most airlines will carry one to two hours of hold fuel, though the FAA does not require the airlines to do so. In terms of cost, the penalty for carrying this fuel is not nearly as great as having to divert to another airport to refuel.

Reserve fuel is the fourth consideration, and the Federal Aviation Regulations (FAR's) dictate a minimum of 45 minutes of reserve fuel. What this means is, if you flew to your destination and circled in a holding pattern waiting for the airport to open, which it never did, then flew to your most distant alternate and landed—when the engines are shut down and passengers deplaned, there will still be a minimum of 45 minutes of fuel in the tanks. Most airlines are more conservative and use a minimum reserve fuel of one hour and fifteen minutes. Ninety-nine percent of the time, there is much more than that, because to land with only reserve fuel assumes you used all your holding fuel at both your primary destination and alternate airport, then flew to the most distant alternate instead of selecting a closer suitable airport to refuel.

Fuel weighs 6.7 pounds per gallon, and the penalty for carrying too much fuel is extra cost. For every one percent the plane's weight is increased, the fuel burn is increased by one and one-half percent. For example, carrying 10,000 pounds (1500 gallons) of extra fuel increases the aircraft's weight such that nearly one-third of that 1500 gallons is used just to carry itself. This is a significant cost.

ALTERNATE COURSES IN CASE OF EMERGENCY OR WEATHER CHANGE

For every flight plan, there is an alternate course in case of emergency.

Visibility requirements for takeoff are generally less restrictive than for landing. Therefore, if the weather is such that a plane can take off from an airport but, in the event of a major malfunction—say, engine failure—could not return to land, there must be a predetermined alternate airport within 320 miles for two-engine aircraft and 700 miles for 3- or 4-engine aircraft.

If there is no alternate airport within the required distance, and the visibility at the point of departure is below minimum landing requirements, the plane will not be allowed to take off.

Landing alternates are also preplanned. There may be

one, two, or more landing alternates selected prior to takeoff, and those might not be the airports closest to the destination. Why? If sixty airplanes were inbound to Dallas–Ft. Worth Airport, and DFW closed, it would be impossible to reroute all sixty to Houston. There wouldn't be enough jetways, fuel trucks, or catering supplies to handle the load.

When the dispatcher plans alternates, he tries to find suitable alternates for every flight. Of course, the pilot has the ultimate say. The captain can, at any time, change the takeoff or landing alternate.

COORDINATING WITH AIR TRAFFIC CONTROL (ATC)

After the calculations have been made to determine the route, fuel load, altitude, and alternate courses of action, a flight plan has to be filed with Air Traffic Control. A specific ATC flight plan is filed for each and every flight.

All flight plans are filed as requests into a central computer at FAA headquarters in Washington, D.C., and they are either approved as filed or amended and returned. Air Traffic Control's main responsibility is traffic separation. Of course, there is a great deal of repetition every day. It's only when weather comes into play that gate-holds, flow-control restrictions, and spacing between aircraft cause delays.

Dispatchers are required to monitor the entire flight, from takeoff delays to arrival. Regular progress reports are made from the pilots directly to the company every hour. A dispatcher is usually required to monitor ten or more flights at a time while continuing to work on upcoming departures.

CHAPTER 2

THE FLIGHT CREW

The flight crew—captains, first officers (co-pilots), second officers (flight engineers), and flight attendants—must sign in at least one hour prior to scheduled departure time for domestic flights, and one and one-half hours for international flights. Signing in on time is particularly critical. If someone fails to show up for work for whatever reason, the flight will have to be postponed until qualified replacements can get to the airport.

There is no juggling of responsibilities. A captain is qualified as a captain on one specific model of aircraft. The co-pilot is qualified as a co-pilot on one specific model of aircraft, etc. A pilot who flies the Boeing 727 is not automatically qualified to fly the Boeing 737, 747, 757, or 767, even though they are all Boeing aircraft. Likewise, a pilot qualified as a first officer (co-pilot) on the 727 is not qualified to fly as the flight engineer or captain without additional training and FAA licensing. All licensing is seat- and aircraft-specific.

PILOT QUALIFICATIONS

First, all cockpit-crew members—captains, first officers, and second officers—are pilots. In the past some airlines employed professional flight engineers who doubled as mechanics. But most have retired, and the need for a mechanic on board has thankfully decreased with the increased reliability of aircraft.

The entry-level position for pilots is the flight engineer's seat, the third pilot in a three-man cockpit. At minimum, a new hire must be a fully FAA-licensed commercial and instrument pilot. A commercial license means a pilot can fly for hire. An instrument pilot's license requires the ability to fly with reference to the flight instruments only. (Quite simply, this pilot can fly in clouds, where there is no outside visibility.) Most pilot new hires are extremely experienced, thirty years of age with 2000 hours experience. They often give up aircraft commander or a higher pilot position with the military, or captain positions with the airline-type commuters. Seniority rules dictate the new hire start at the most junior flight position.

After an extensive four- to six-week second-officer course specific to one airplane; written and oral exams; simulator and airplane check rides; a new pilot is licensed to be a flight engineer. Further, to qualify to "fly the line"— meaning engineer an airplane with passengers—a new hire must pass a line check by an FAA-designated check airman who supervises his performance for the first 25 hours in his new position.

Pilots can bid for more senior positions as positions become available through FAA mandatory retirement (which is age sixty) or airline expansion. If a new hire elects transition from second officer on the Boeing 727 to second officer on a Lockheed 1011 or DC-10 for example, it's back to school for another month—more exams, simulator checkrides, and line checks.

Upgrade training is similar to transition training in

length and comprehension, except that it means you are changing "seats" on an aircraft, upgrading flight engineer to first officer, or first officer to captain. If you are upgrading from F/E to F/O after passing the FAA-required exam and checkrides, the same 25 hours of supervised flying is required. However, upgrading to captain is more involved.

To be a captain on an airline, you must have an FAA Air Transport Pilot's License. It can be confusing, because many people refer to airline pilots as commercial pilots when all captains and many co-pilots hold their ATP certificate.

Starting at the beginning, the first license a pilot can earn is a Private Pilot License allowing him to fly passengers, but not fly them for money. To fly for hire you need to qualify for the Commercial Pilots License, most commonly with an Instrument Rating (fly in clouds). Next is the Air Transport Pilots License, requiring a minimum of 1500 hours' flight experience just to sit for the exams and checkrides. It's the Ph.D. of aviation.

Most pilots have far more experience than that. With the established carriers, starting as a flight engineer and progressing to co-pilot and then captain can take up to twelve or more years. By then somewhere between 10,000 to 15,000 hours have been accumulated—again, much more than the FAA requires.

A nonairline pilot can earn an ATP. Indeed, most corporate and charter pilots have them, though the ATP alone is not enough to captain an air transport. For airplanes weighing more than 12,500 pounds—the size of a commuter and heavier—you need a type rating specific to the airplane. Therefore, to be an airline captain, you need both the ATP license and type rating.

Completing all the required checks is a fairly intensive experience. If you fail, say, on a highly computerized new technology airplane, and then elect to transition back to your old equipment, in most cases you have to requalify on the original airplane again. Assuming you pass the written, the company oral, the FAA oral; the simulator checks testing your ability to handle all normal, abnormal, and emergency procedures; the airplane flight check with no passengers, and the 25 hours of supervised flying with passengers; you still only qualify as a High Minimum Captain.

High Minimum Captain is a fancy term for new captain. For the first 300 hours, a new captain is governed by more conservative weather conditions than somebody with more experience, despite whatever experience has been logged in the co-pilot's seat. A new pilot, then, cannot land in low or dense fog or in certain other significant weather—at least for the first 300 hours. When a captain qualifies for a different airplane, the restrictions are then only 100 hours. These days, computers track crew assignments in order to prevent new captains and new co-pilots from flying together. If such a match-up occurs, it's their responsibility to notify crew scheduling, which then notifies dispatch, and a crew swap is made.

Every six months pilots are "line checked" for continuing proficiency of normal operating procedures by the FAA or designated check pilot. Also, every six months pilots are "simulator" checked for proficiency in all normal, abnormal, and emergency procedures. Pilots are also required to have medical check-ups every six months by an FAA-approved aeromedical flight surgeon. Failing a physical for any ailment, no matter how minor, means you are "grounded" and cannot fly.

FLIGHT SIMULATORS

The use of full-motion, full-scale flight simulators has greatly improved pilot training. More training can be accomplished in less time and, in some cases, with more realism than in the actual airplane. For example, practicing an engine fire emergency on takeoff is impossible in a real aircraft without damaging the engine. In a flight simulator the computer can be programmed to accurately portray a real engine fire and the resultant flight characteristics caused by the failure of one or more engines. During the emergency, how well the simulator "flies" depends on the emergency action and proficiency of the pilots.

Every conceivable airplane malfunction, including multiple engine failures, hydraulic failures, electrical failures, pressurization failures, landing gear malfunctions, etc. can be practiced over and over to sharpen your skills.

Punch a few more buttons and the instructor can simulate poor weather conditions such as dense fog, ice, snow, turbulence, and even windshear, regardless of the real outside weather.

FLIGHT ATTENDANTS

The requirement is a minimum of one flight attendant for every fifty seats. If there are 175 seats, there must be a minimum of four flight attendants. It doesn't matter if the plane is empty or full. Most airlines, however, use more flight attendants than the minimum because the airline industry is an extremely service-oriented business.

DO CREWS WORK TOGETHER OFTEN?

Not always. Flight crews generally bid for regular trips and work together for an entire month. However, when one crew member has requalification training, a simulator checkride, vacation, or is sick, a substitution is made, and crew members might be meeting for the first time when they sign in.

PILOT RESTRICTIONS

When crew members sign-in—specifically the captain, co-pilot, and engineer—they are putting their FAA licenses on the line by agreeing that:

1. They are not using medication of any kind. Special FAA aeromedical approval is required to take medi-

cation of any sort, including over-the-counter cough suppressant or allergy tablets. Major medication for maladies such as blood pressure would prevent certification in the first place.

2. They have not ingested any alcohol. Until recently it was against the law to drink alcohol less than eight hours before departure. Added to this today is the requirement that, regardless of the time, your body should be alcohol-free to safely fly. If the obvious safety issues and criminal penalties are not enough, the airlines will fire the offender as well as terminate the other flight-crew members for not preventing the abuser from flying. Crew members have been subject to random drug testing since December 1989.

3. They certify that they've not gone scuba diving or donated blood within twenty-four hours.

4. Because of the concern of food poisoning within six hours of takeoff, the captain and first officer cannot eat the same meal from the same kitchen.

5. When signing in, pilots are also certifying they are not violating any FAA-mandated fatigue restrictions. Because it can take nearly two hours of work ("duty time") for every one hour of actual flight time, the Federal Aviation Regulations stipulate for safety that a pilot may not fly more than 30 hours in seven consecutive days, more than 100 hours in a calendar month, and more than 1000 hours in a calendar year. These are flight-time hours, not total on-the-job "duty" hours.

6. Finally, when signing in, crew members must have in possession their FAA license, medical certificate, and their FAA radio-telephone license.

REVIEWING THE WORK OF DISPATCH

With ultimate authority and responsibility for the flight, the pilot in command and the co-pilot begin the process of double-checking dispatch.

First, they pull up all significant weather information, scanning the forecasts, the winds, and surface weather. Then they survey the dispatcher's preliminary flight plan and check his weather reports, the fuel allotment, the amount of trip fuel and how much hold fuel. The pilot then compares that information with previous experience. Any disagreement, and the pilot can request changes, no questions asked.

PILOT'S FLIGHT KIT

Flight kits—the big, heavy briefcaselike bags pilots carry —contain the Pilot's Operating Manual, all normal and abnormal procedures, the Pilot's Reference Manual, charts, diagrams, and descriptions of the individual aircraft system, and the Pilot's Navigational Charts. These books contain all the published normal and abnormal procedures. When changes are made, charts and information are revised.

The most frequently revised documents are the Jeppesen Navigational Charts (charts made by a private company in Denver, Colorado, with information supplied by the FAA). These contain all routes necessary to fly—from where airport gates are located to the SIDS and STARS. They also publish low and high altitude en route charts, terminal charts, and area charts. Revisions come out every two weeks.

More frequent changes are also delivered in NOTAMS— notices to airmen. Special bulletins about airports, such as new construction or maintenance, and temporary faults with FAA-monitored navigational aids, are highlighted.

CHAPTER 3

THE AIRCRAFT: EXTERIOR AND SAFETY

Aircraft are scheduled for 45 minutes to one hour ground time between flights, during which time they are cleaned and serviced. While the passenger service agent meets the flight and confirms with the flight attendants the number of extra-assistance passengers—wheelchair, elderly, unaccompanied minor children, non-English speaking—the first person to talk with the inbound flight crew is an FAA-licensed mechanic.

WHAT THE MECHANIC DOES

If the flight crew detected any type of mechanical malfunction while in the air—from a generator tripping off line to the movie being improperly projected—they will have radioed the problem to the maintenance coordinator via central dispatch. The maintenance coordinator will in turn contact the local mechanics, who will meet the flight with the tools needed to replace the malfunctioning part. The airlines have found it more timely to replace parts than repair them. After removal from the plane, the faulty part can be shipped to a central maintenance hangar and rebuilt like-new. Once repaired, it can be returned to the "on line" inventory.

If a problem occurs closer to the airport—on approach, for instance—there isn't time to radio the maintenance coordinator and discuss it. In this case, when the mechanic meets the inbound plane, he'll find out about the problem by plugging his headset into an interphone jack located near the nose wheel and asking the flight crew, "How's the aircraft?"

Whenever there is something wrong with the plane, it must be legally noted in an aircraft log book. The log book is kept on the airplane at all times, and it contains that plane's mechanical history. This enables the crew to anticipate a problem before it happens. Also, if something recurs frequently, the plane will be taken out of service and repaired.

Most frequently, nothing is wrong and the mechanic will begin the first of two walkarounds—or inspections—of the airplane. A member of the flight crew conducts the other one. The mechanic begins the exterior inspection while the passengers are still deplaning, then comes to the cockpit to check the pressure and quantities of oil, hydraulics, fuel, and emergency oxygen.

On the newer aircraft the mechanic can directly access the aircraft's "status" computers. These computers record transient malfunctions, discrepancies that are not displayed on the cockpit instruments and engine exceedences. With these status computers, troubleshooting becomes more efficient and cost-effective.

When the mechanic is satisfied the plane is airworthy, he will sign the log book, deeming the plane okay for its next flight.

FLIGHT CREW WALKAROUND

The pilots are required to arrive at the airplane thirty minutes prior to departure. Responsibility for the flight crews' walkaround, which follows on the heels of the mechanic's inspection, will usually fall on the junior member—the co-pilot if it's a two-man crew, the flight engineer if there are three.

WHAT IS CHECKED DURING THE WALKAROUND INSPECTION?

The exterior inspection of an aircraft is a general condition check and an inspection of more than 100 specific items. The airplane's exterior surface is checked for dents and peeling paint, or any possible signs of damage or wear. If some damage is found, for instance a dent, an airframe mechanic would inspect the area to determine if the plane can remain in service or if a more detailed inspection and repair is necessary.

Specific checks include a visual inspection of the exterior components (discussed later in this chapter) with extra attention given to the high-use items such as the landing gear, brakes, and tires. The multiple hydraulic systems are checked for minute leaks, particularly around the pumps and actuators, where a drip can be detected before it registers on the cockpit gauges. The engines are checked for visible wear and the presence of oil in non-normal locations. The fuel lines, which are encased in a protective sleeve, are checked for leaks at these sleeve drain ports. Flight controls are checked and their position is noted. They are later verified with the cockpit flight-control position gauges. Pressurization valves are inspected. Ram-air and static-air vents are examined to ensure that they are open and clear. Service and inspection panels are all checked to be properly closed and locked.

ICE AND FROST

During the cold winter months a thorough preflight inspection must include checking for frost or ice on the wings. If there is any, or if the pilot thinks there's a possibility it might form, then the airplane must be de-iced. De-icing is done with de-icing fluids. The Type One fluid, the original type solution, is good for fifteen minutes. The Type Two fluid, a newer one, is good for thirty minutes or more. Ice or frost on the wings reduces the lifting capability and adds weight, and therefore must be removed before takeoff.

The aircraft has its own anti-ice system on board. The engine anti-ice system can be used full-time, and when needed can be turned on immediately after engine start. The wing anti-ice system gets its hot-air supply from the engine compressors, and if used on the ground, would reduce the power available for takeoff. Consequently, this system is not used until the plane is at least 400 feet above ground and climbing.

If a plane is de-iced at the gate and, for some reason, there is a lengthy delay at the runway, it is necessary for the wings to be reinspected for ice and frost. If there is a renewed buildup, the plane must return to the gate again.

Airlines are now beginning to experiment with a new "car wash" approach to de-icing. Instead of de-icing at the gate, a specific de-icing facility located on a taxiway near the active runway provides de-icing closer to departure time. This system requires the aircraft climate-control system must be turned off for up to five minutes to prevent the smell of the de-icing fluid from entering the cabin. The disadvantages are: (1) The plane's interior would get cold; and (2) de-icing away from the gate doesn't allow the flight crew to completely inspect their own aircraft, since not all of the plane can be seen from inside the cockpit and cabin.

WHAT ELSE IS GOING ON DURING THE WALKAROUND?

As the crew member conducts the walkaround, he is surrounded by a flurry of activity. A fuel truck. A catering truck. Conveyor belts used to load the individual luggage, mechanized loaders for the container luggage and cargo, plus all the tugs and carts needed to haul everything. A water-servicing truck to refill the drinking water tanks. A waste truck, which suctions out the holding tanks. And any kind of maintenance vehicles necessary to work on the plane. The aircraft are designed so that the various vehicles can all work at the same time.

EXTERIOR AIRCRAFT COMPONENTS

Looking out at a plane from the terminal does not always do justice to the size of the aircraft. Take one of the newer jets, the Boeing 767–300. The airplane is 180 feet long, which is about two-thirds of a football field. Its highest point measures 52 feet, about five stories. The wing span, from tip to tip, is 156 feet, a length that would extend across more than ten lanes of an interstate. At 24 feet, 4 inches, the cockpit is almost two stories above the ground. The diameter of the airplane itself is 16 feet, 6 inches.

Some airlines paint their planes, others don't. The basic choice comes down to personal preferences, but there are advantages to painting the craft. Paint helps prevent corrosion and can help cool the fuselage during hot summer months. The major disadvantage of paint is it's weight. An L-1011, for instance, has over 8,632 square feet of painted area, which requires roughly 58 gallons of paint weighing almost 700 pounds.

THE ENGINES

The powerful engines are perhaps the most ominous-looking feature of an airplane. The two engines on a 767 are 106 inches in diameter—that's 8 feet, 10 inches, taller than many of the rooms in your home, and larger than the diameter of the fuselage of the original DC-3 manufactured in the 1930s and 1940s. Each of those engines weighs more than 10,000 pounds. That's five tons. The 767 uses two of these engines; the MD-11, a heavier airplane, three; and the 747–400, still bigger, four.

Not surprisingly, the engines are as powerful as they are large. Each engine is capable of generating 60,000 pounds of thrust, which is 24,000 horsepower. An older 727 has three engines, each developing 15,500 pounds of thrust. For comparison, one 767 engine is more powerful than all three of a 727's combined.

ENGINE RELIABILITY

Two assumptions are usually made about engine reliability, and both are false. One, that as engines get bigger and more powerful, they become more susceptible to failure. Two, as engines become older, they are more likely to have breakdowns. Neither is true.

Engines in service are meticulously maintained and regularly overhauled back to like-new status. And unlike your automobile, as advancements are made in engine technology, some of these improvements can be incorporated on an older engine during overhaul. In reality, some of the older engines, after modifications and refinements, are just now achieving the level of reliability of the newer turbofan engines. Statistically speaking, the chances of an engine shutdown—whether as a precaution or actual malfunction, are approximately one per 50,000 hours of flight time. (Though this is extremely remote, we will discuss later how all aircraft are designed and all pilots are trained and retrained for the worst-case scenario.)

FUEL

To most people, wings appear thin and narrow. Nothing could be further from the truth. Most of the airplane's fuel is stored inside the wings. Why? It adds extra strength. If you squeeze a full carton of milk, it is less compressible than a carton that's empty. Likewise, aircraft wings filled with fuel are stronger.

How much fuel is contained? A 767, for example, holds 24,000 gallons of fuel. That may not sound like a lot, but there is enough fuel on board a 767 to operate your car for 32 years. The 747–400, the largest plane in commercial use, holds 60,000 gallons of fuel, an amount that would enable you to run the family car for 80 years.

THE WINGS

Passengers often ask if the wings are large and strong enough to support the entire airframe through all types of weather over years of service. The answer is yes.

The size of a wing is directly proportional to the maximum weight of the airplane. The wing of the 747–400, which has a surface area greater than a basketball court, has to support exactly the same weight per square foot (100 pounds) as the wing of a smaller airplane with a smaller wing. The wings are made out of two giant steel girders, the same type of girders used in high-rise buildings. Two of these girders extend from tip to tip through a wing box that is attached to the fuselage. Essentially, that's the structure of the wing itself. They are incredibly strong, but also incredibly flexible—like buildings that have the strength and flexibility to sway and bend and not crumble during earthquakes or extremely high winds.

In fact, in normal flight the wings flex 3 to 6 feet. Maximum flexibility tolerance greatly exceeds that. In the case of a 747, the wings are stressed to flex 29 feet up and down without damage. The strength of the wing and fuselage are equally impressive. Aircraft are built to withstand a minimum of 2½ g's—or more than 2½ times the force of gravity. What does this mean? One g of gravity is the force we feel normally here on earth. If we could fly into space, we would feel zero g's, or be weightless. A 767, for example, has a maximum gross weight of 407,000 pounds. When there is turbulence putting stress on the airframe and wings, the plane is constructed to withstand 2½ times that 407,000 pounds. The manufacturers are also required to build the aircraft to withstand an additional 50 percent safety overload above the already conservative maximum stress limit. What this means is that the wings of a plane with a gross weight of 407,000 pounds can support well over one million pounds of weight in normal flight, and 1½ million pounds in a maximum-stress condition.

SLATS/FLAPS

Slats are a series of panels on the front side—or leading edge—of the wing. They can be symmetrically moved forward and down. The *flaps* are two sets of panels located along the backside or trailing edge of the wings. They can move outward and downward. At the gate on most aircraft the flaps and slats are positioned in the fully up, or retracted, position. Both slats and flaps are operated hydraulically but locked (held in position) mechanically. On the underside of the wings you can see the cover for the jack screws that turn to move the flaps.

When the flaps and slats are fully extended they increase the surface area approximately 20 percent and the lifting capability of the wings 80 percent. What this does, in simple terms, is make it possible for the plane to fly slower, which reduces the amount of runway needed for takeoff and landing.

If for some reason there was a malfunction and the flight crew couldn't get the flaps and slats out hydraulically, they would turn to a backup electrical system. If those failed, there are further redundant systems that would enable them to bypass the faulty portion of the system and extend some of the flaps and slats. But in the extremely rare situation where nothing could be done, the plane could still land. The only difference is that the crew would have to land at a higher speed, requiring a longer runway and utilizing greater braking power after touchdown.

COMPASSES, GYROS, AND STROBES

All aircraft have compasses on board, even though the old-fashioned Boy Scout navigational tools are rarely used. Their shortcoming is that they are susceptible to magnetic and radio interference common in an airplane. Instead, directional gyroscopes or heading indicators are used. This directional system uses sensors that are located in the wing tips as far from any interference as possible, with their compass display located in the cockpit. To further reduce the interference, the wing tips are made of a nonmetal graphite epoxy, which is a slightly different color than the rest of the plane. They are secured with demagnetized screws.

Also found on the wing tips are position lights. The left wing tip has a red light, the right one a green light. Mounted on the rear of the wing tips are white lights. They are on continually, day and night, and assist in helping the flight crew tell if a plane is coming toward them or flying away.

Also on the wing tips are white strobe lights. The strobes flash 48 times a minute, and they're used as an anticollision light. When flying through clouds, their reflection into the passenger cabin can sometimes be mistaken for lightning.

Additionally, on the top and bottom of the fuselage not

directly visible from the cabin, there is a flashing red rotating beacon—also an anticollision light. Though not as bright as a strobe in clouds, the red reflection is sometimes visible.

AILERONS

These are one or two sets of movable surfaces on the trailing edge of the wings, used to control the angle of bank when making turns. When one aileron goes up during a turn, the other simultaneously goes down. The result is unequal lift on the two wings, causing the aircraft to bank, and thus turn.

SPEED BRAKES AND SPOILERS

These are the multiple large panels that rise from the trailing-edge portion of the top of the wings. In the air they're called *speed brakes,* and on the ground the same panels function as *spoilers.* The left-wing and right-wing panels can be moved independently from the cockpit to augment the roll or turning capability of the aircraft. Using a speed brake handle located between the captain and co-pilot, both the left and right set of panels can be used simultaneously to slow the plane down.

When Air Traffic Control asks a pilot to descend and slow down at the same time, the speed brakes are deployed. If you were going downhill in your car and just took your foot off the gas, there wouldn't be a huge difference in speed. Same thing with an airplane. So these panels actually rise above the wing, causing an increase in drag and enabling the plane to slow down at the same time it descends.

In the air they come up in increments to a maximum of 40 degrees; on the ground they go up rapidly to 60 degrees, instantly spoiling lift, decreasing the chances of a bounce on landing, and applying extra weight on the landing gear to increase braking effectiveness.

THE LANDING GEAR—TIRES

The piece of equipment on an airplane that receives the most wear and tear are the tires. Aircraft tires do not rotate in the air, therefore, at touchdown the tires spin up from zero to the landing speed of almost 150 mph instantly. Watching aircraft land, you can see the puff of smoke generated when touchdown and simultaneous wheel spin-up occurs.

The tires are extremely durable. The tires on a 767 are up to 32 ply, a drastic increase over the two- or four-ply tires of a family car. If there is a single nick or tear in just an outermost layer, the 32nd ply, the tire will be replaced. Under normal wear and tear, tires are changed every 200 or so landings—about every month and a half.

The tire pressure is 220 pounds per square inch, and during the walkaround, if pressure is ever found to be as little as 20 pounds low, instead of troubleshooting the cause, the tire is automatically replaced.

Replacing a tire is no small task. A sixty-ton (120,000 pound) hydraulic jack lifts the landing gear section of the tire being replaced off the ground, and a one-ton hydraulic lift is used just to lift the tires into position. A tire change can be completed on a fully loaded aircraft.

One hundred eighty-five pounds of tire pressure seems high to those of us used to filling our auto tires with 25 pounds of air. But it's quite important when you consider hydroplaning, a condition in rainy weather when a film of moisture can build up between the runway and the tires, reducing the frictional contact with the pavement.

There's a specific formula used to figure out when a tire will hydroplane. It's nine times the square root of the tire pressure. If a car tire is inflated to 25 pounds per square inch, the speed at which the car will hydroplane is 45 mph.

For an airplane, whose tires are filled to 220 psi, it's 133 mph. The chances of hydroplaning on a wet runway are further reduced by use of the ground spoilers to spoil lift and increase the effective weight on the tires. By crowning and grooving the runway—higher in the center, with channels every several inches to enhance water runoff— even during heavy rain, water buildup is kept to a minimum.

The tires themselves are inflated with dry nitrogen—not air—to reduce their flammability in case the tires got excessively hot. The tires are also equipped with heat-sensitive fuse plugs, which blow out when the tire's internal temperature rises above a certain point—usually greater than 350 degrees. When these plugs blow out, they release pressure slowly, preventing a sudden blowout that could effect directional control at high speeds on the runways or be a safety hazard to personnel in the ramp area.

The crew monitors these temperatures in the cockpit on a brake temperature gauge that warns of hot brakes causing hot tires.

The tires have a maximum speed of 253 mph, far above what's required for normal takeoff and landings.

THE BRAKES

Each tire has its own set of brakes. But unlike a car's brakes—one disc per tire—a plane will usually have five or more sets of discs for each tire. Therefore, on one wheel assembly with four tires, there will be four sets of brakes with twenty stopping discs.

The amount of energy absorbed by the brakes during the deceleration after landing is enormous. Heat can build up rapidly. On a warm summer day, after a landing with only moderate braking, it can take 30 to 45 minutes for the brakes to cool down to the ambient outside temperature. Since most flights are scheduled for at least a 45-minute ground turnaround time, this brake cooling period does not usually cause a delay.

Each brake also has a brake-wear pin, which is checked on the walkaround. The pin protrudes from the brake assembly. When the brake wears down, the brake pad thins and causes the pin to retract. When it gets to a certain point, the brakes are changed. Under a new FAA rule, all aircraft stopping distances are calculated assuming only 10 percent of each brake's pad is remaining. So even as the brake pads wear, the stopping capability of your airplane will be better than the test aircraft.

Older type brakes are made of metal. Though extremely reliable, they could under extreme heat conditions lose some effectiveness. They could also heat up to a point that if you applied your parking brake once stopped at the gate, the brakes could "lock-up," which requires a complete brake change. All new aircraft are equipped with carbon disc brakes, which are able to dissipate the heat faster, reducing brake cooling times and the risk of locked brakes at the gate.

Looking at an aircraft at the gate, you will see large rubber or metal "chocks" in front and behind all the tires. Though there is little chance an aircraft would roll on level ground, by using these chocks as a safety against ground movement, the flight crew does not have to leave the parking brake on at the gate. Brake cooling is much more effective with the parking brake off.

In addition, each brake has its own antiskid system similar to an automobile's antilock system. If the brakes were applied and the antiskid system sensed the wheels were not turning, due possibly to a skid, the system would automatically release the brakes, allow the tire to spin up and instantaneously reapply brake pressure. In the case where one individual brake on one tire—say, the left side—was grabbing, the antiskid system would release that brake as well as the one brake on the right-side tire assembly simultaneously, to prevent directional control problems. All other individual brakes would function normally.

AUXILIARY POWER UNIT

The Auxiliary Power Unit (APU) is located in the tail of most aircraft. The APU is a jet engine, about the size of an engine found on most commuter aircraft. It provides for ground electricity and air for ground air conditioning, but no thrust.

If you ever walk the ramp area of a commercial airport, you will hear the tremendous jet engine noise generated by the APU.

FLIGHT AND VOICE RECORDERS

The flight and voice recorders that are always mentioned any time there is an accident are also located in the tail. Though commonly called the black boxes, they are housed in bright orange containers, which are able to withstand incredible forces—200 g's or more—and incredibly high temperatures—+2000 degrees Farenheit. They are located in the tail for maintenance accessibility.

Inside the flight recorder there is a 25-hour tape that records all the parameters of the flight, including the time, altitude, airspeed, vertical acceleration, heading, the time of each radio transmission, the pitch and roll of the plane, the position of the flight controls, position of the thrust levers and the thrust (power) of each engine, the flap position, and so on.

The voice recorder is separate and records all cockpit conversations and radio transmissions with ATC and the company.

Both recording devices are automatically activated whenever the aircraft is operating and has electrical power. If an airplane was forced to ditch at sea, the flight recorder contains a water-activated transmitter that will emit signals for thirty days to aid in its recovery.

NOSE WHEEL ASSEMBLY

The nose wheels, the two front tires, are the only steer-able wheels of an aircraft. Using a tiller, or side-mounted steering wheel in the cockpit, the nose gear can turn approximately 75 degrees left or right of center, allowing for almost perfect corner turns. Though not a landing gear per se, the nose wheel is extremely strong and is the point at which the ground service tug attaches to the aircraft for pushback from the gate.

Also located on or near the nose-wheel assembly is a ground-alert system. Some of the same horns and buzzers that sound in the cockpit—indicating, for example, the electronic equipment bay is not being cooled or the APU is overheating—will sound at the nose-wheel area, alerting the ground crew to investigate a problem, if the flight crew hasn't already arrived.

NOSE

The nose of the aircraft is called the *radome.* Painted a nonreflective color, usually black, in order to reduce glare in the cockpit, the radome is made of nonmetallic plexi-glass and houses the weather radar. The radar scans up to 320 miles in front of the aircraft, left and right almost 90 degrees, up and down nearly 15 degrees, and it can detect rain showers, thunderstorms, and their associated turbulence.

COCKPIT WINDOWS

From the outside, the cockpit windows appear small, especially in relation to the airplane's overall size. But when you're sitting in the cockpit, you're close to the windows and the visibility is excellent. As technology for window strength improves, the cockpit windows on newer airplanes are getting larger.

The windshield is obviously much stronger than a car's. It's built of three layers of glass and separated by two layers of vinyl. It's almost three-quarters of an inch thick. The windows are electrically heated, which prevents buildups of fog and ice, and also reduces brittleness in the very cold climates of high altitude.

The windows are individually heated by two systems. If the heating systems all failed, the airplane's cruise speed would be reduced until a repair could be made at the next station. Any imperfections in the windshield affecting its strength would dictate windshield replacement immediately.

Although there's quite a bit of pressure pushing on the window from the outside when traveling 550 mph, there is also 8.6 psi of internal pressure pushing from the inside out. A balance is struck. This enhances window strength. Window strength is tested by the manufacturers with a five-inch boregun. Objects are shot at the forward fuselage and windows; the only acceptable mark is no damage at all.

PASSENGER WINDOWS

The cabin windows are double paned for extra strength. The plastic shield you can touch from the cabin is not part of the window structure but simply a temperature and moisture barrier. The size and location of the cabin windows are dictated by the structure of the aircraft itself. Windows are rounded at the corners to reduce points of structural stress.

CHAPTER 4

THE AIRCRAFT: INTERIOR AND SAFETY

GETTING ON THE AIRPLANE

Anyone who's ever boarded an airplane knows well that these aircraft are so vast it's nearly impossible to see from front to rear. When it comes right down to it, the dimensions are imposing. The interior of a 767 is 133 feet long, the ceiling is 9 feet, 5 inches, and there's a total of 1981 square feet—better than an average-sized house. The inside of a 747 is even larger—3529 square feet. But to fully appreciate how enormous these widebody planes are, consider: The Wright brother's entire first flight, from takeoff through cruise and then landing, could have been completed inside one of these giant airplanes.

THE DOORS

You board a plane usually through one of two doors, the forward or the mid-cabin entry door.

All the doors on an aircraft—the entry and galley doors, emergency exits, over-wing exits—are plug-type doors.

What this means is that the door itself is larger than the fuselage opening. These doors are primarily secured with metal bolts and latches, but what makes them impossible to open in flight is the internal cabin pressure that firmly plugs the doors in place.

On widebody aircraft, the plug doors open inward and upward into the ceiling. They have primary electric systems and a spring-loaded backup. On narrow-body aircraft, where the curve of the airplane doesn't leave enough space for the door to be stowed in the overhead area, the doors open inward—remember, they are larger than the opening —then slightly fold and rotate outward through the opening.

THE NUMBER OF DOORS

The number of doors and emergency exits on an airplane are specifically dictated by FAA regulations. Doors, including emergency and over-wing exits, can't be more than 60 feet apart. From any seat in the plane you would have to move no more than 30 feet to reach an exit. This calculation is based on a worst-case scenario. In the event of an emergency evacuation, for whatever reason, if half the doors were unusable or blocked, the entire load of passengers could still be evacuated within 90 seconds.

ARMED AND CROSS-CHECKED DOORS

All doors have a two-position lever, which, when turned one way or another, makes them either *armed* or *unarmed.* Often on pushback, passengers hear the flight attendants say, "Armed and cross-checked." What they're doing is arming the automatic escape or evacuation slides. These slides are located within the doors themselves. If a door slide is armed and the emergency handle is pulled, the door will move out of the closed position and the escape slides will deploy. This can't happen in the air because once the plane is pressurized, moving the handle and opening the door is impossible.

SEATS

Each seat is flash and fire resistant. So are the carpets, ceilings, and any other upholstered surface on board the plane. Every seat is required to have a seat belt. If it doesn't, or if it doesn't work, that seat can't be occupied. The tray tables must fully retract and lock for the seat to be usable. The seat back doesn't necessarily have to recline, but must stay locked upright to be used.

Additionally, these seats all have what is mislabeled a breakaway feature. Not that they come off the floor or break apart. What this means is that if the plane were making an emergency landing and the passengers were in emergency landing position—head between knees and braced with arms—the seat in front of you will, on impact, give about six to eight inches. In other words, the seat back will move forward from the upright position and absorb some of the force.

It has never been proven that seats in one section of an airplane are safer than another. But there are little things to note. The plane is most stable near its center of gravity, the midsection. Aircraft are quieter if you can sit in front of the engines. Most have engines on the wings, so it's going to be somewhat quieter in front. Aircraft could be built to be almost completely soundproof—however, acoustic studies have proven that the background noise from the engines helps dampen the sound of conversations, making multiple conversations possible without generating the noise level of an auditorium.

The first row of any section—the first row behind what's called the bulkhead—has slightly more leg room. The same with emergency-exit rows. Window seats are good for viewing, aisle seats for getting up and walking around. For those who want to sleep on a long flight, it's important to know that seats in the first row behind any bulkhead have tray tables in the armrests, which prevents them from being raised.

The window seat immediately in front of an over-wing exit—the row directly in front of the emergency exits—doesn't recline. If it did, it would block the exit. No more than one infant is allowed in a single row. This is because there's only one extra oxygen mask per row.

If you don't select a seat for yourself, the computer will automatically do so. The computers are programmed to randomly seat passengers throughout the airplane in a way that provides maximum comfort and the most even distribution of weight.

OVERHEAD BINS

According to FAA regulations, passengers may not take on board more than two pieces of carry-on baggage, excluding purses, diaper bags, camera cases, and umbrellas. There are two reasons for this:

1. Central load control, which calculates the exact weight and balance of the plane before each flight, must make weight assumptions regarding carry-on luggage. To make these estimates as accurate as possible, the FAA imposes a two-piece limit.
2. Since all carry-on luggage must fit underneath a seat or in an overhead bin, so as not to restrict your ability to quickly evacuate in an emergency, the two-piece limit is proportional to how much cabin storage is available. Since many passengers prefer to carry on their luggage rather than check it, the new aircraft are being built with more than 2½ cubic feet of overhead storage area per passenger.

ENTERTAINMENT SYSTEMS

On aircraft designed for longer flights, each individual seat has its own entertainment system. On the latest generation of airplanes, these entertainment systems are wireless. Each seat has its own receiver to pick up the audio-visual signals for the music and movie. The weight savings of the equipment and associated wires justifies the added cost of the equipment.

LIGHTS AND FANS

The reading lights above the seats are individually controlled. If a bulb is not working, they can be changed.

Above each seat is a fan outlet. Cold air from the aircraft gasper fan can be used to adjust the temperature around your seat. Some are manually opened and closed, others operate from a push button in your armrest.

FOOD AND BEVERAGES

A major airline has approximately 2500 flights serving 150,000 passengers a day. This translates into 130,000 meals and snacks, 375,000 beverages, of which 133,000 are coffee and tea, 40,000 cocktails, 186,000 soft drinks, and 16,000 glasses of wine and champagne each and every day. To chill these beverages takes 105,000 pounds of ice daily.

According to one carrier, a fully-provisioned 747 holds 491 cups, 972 plates, 847 glasses, 176 bottles of wine, and 25 gallons of liquor.

LAVATORIES

The number of toilets is dictated by the capacity of the airplane and the assumption that one-quarter of all passengers will use the bathroom every hour. Passengers new to flying are sometimes alarmed by the noise of the toilets. Since all waste is remotely stored in one or more holding tanks, which hold 120 gallons each, a rather substantial 4½ horsepower flushing motor is required for toilet operation. By comparison, a push-type home lawnmower is about two horsepower. Since these flush motors use electrical power and are subject to wear and tear, above 16,000 feet cabin pressure differential is used instead. Using just seven ounces of water, waste is literally sucked to the holding tanks. No waste is ever dumped overboard. The waste tanks are emptied between flights.

FIRE SAFETY EQUIPMENT

Each of the airplane's galleys is equipped with a traditional fire extinguisher, a water and anti-freeze mix pressurized with carbon dioxide housed in a green bottle. These are for paper-type fires and their use is limited.

The most adaptable fire extinguishers, stored in red fire bottles, are Halon fire extinguishers. These are pressurized liquefied gas extinguishers. The Halon extinguishers are good on all types of fires, including electrical, fuel, grease, and paper.

To prevent smoke inhalation while fighting an on-board fire, all planes are equipped with protective breathing equipment. These hoodlike devices fit over the head, providing fifteen minutes of oxygen and thermal protection, enabling crew members to fight a fire from closer range.

FIRST-AID KITS

Airplanes are stocked with standard first-aid kits, which are checked and, if necessary, restocked before every departure. These kits include: antiseptic swabs, burn ointments, compress bandages, scissors, regular bandages, ammonia inhalants, splints, adhesive tape, CPR masks with one-way breathing valves, as well as other items normally found in such kits. They are located throughout the cabin.

MEDICAL KITS

This is relatively new. But the FAA now requires all airplanes to have emergency medical kits on board. The medical kit is stored in the cockpit and is only to be used by a fully licensed medical doctor. It is illegal for any of the flight crew, from pilot to flight attendants, to open this kit. Inside, there's a blood pressure cuff, stethoscope, alcohol swabs, some prescription medication, syringes, needles, nitroglycerin tablets, tourniquets, and surgical gloves.

Any medical emergency that would require use of the medical kit would, with the consultation of a doctor on board, cause the pilot to declare the flight a medical emergency. In the event of an emergency, the captain could call the flight a lifeguard flight, to automatically receive priority handling. Additionally, in a life-threatening situation, the captain would alter the flight plan to land at the nearest suitable airport that could provide appropriate medical support.

DEPRESSURIZATION

All aircraft have multiple pressurization systems: one or two automatic systems, a standby system, and a manual backup. In the statistically improbable event they all failed at once, you would experience a slow depressurization because the airplane can be made airtight. In all likelihood, the flight crew would be able to descend even before any supplemental oxygen would be needed.

The rapid depressurization is what would catch our attention. Let's take a worst-case scenario. Say a large hole was blown in the side of the fuselage. First, all aircraft are required to be built so that if the fuselage sustained a 20-square-foot hole, the plane would still be flyable. Manufacturers routinely double that figure to 40 square feet to provide extra protection.

Second, if there was an explosive depressurization, the cabin pressure inside would equalize the cabin pressure outside almost instantly. Passengers sitting immediately adjacent to a large explosive hole and not wearing their seat belts would be lost, but milliseconds later the risk to everyone else would diminish to zero.

What would happen in such a scenario? After hearing a fairly loud noise, there would be a very rapid cooling and fogging of the air caused by the very cold outside air mixing with the warm cabin air. Your ears might pop or feel blocked from the rapid pressure change. The flight crew would begin a rapid descent to 14,000 or below while you donned your emergency oxygen mask. Two to three minutes later you would be in warmer, breathable air, and the crew would proceed to the nearest suitable airport.

EMERGENCY OXYGEN

At cruising altitudes above 14,000 feet it is an FAA requirement to carry on-board supplemental oxygen. The reason: as the plane ascends, even though the percentage of oxygen in the air remains the same, the pressure of the air decreases. At 18,000 feet the pressure of the atmosphere is half that of sea level, and it decreases further with altitude. For this reason, aircraft are pressurized to maintain a normal breathing atmosphere. At normal cruising altitudes the air inside the cabin is pressurized to a comfortable 7000 feet. What this means is, with the airplane flying at 35,000 feet you will feel like you are at 7000 feet. For comparison, Denver, Colorado, is 5300 feet, and most mountain towns in the Sierra and Rocky Mountains are much higher.

In the unlikely event of a cabin depressurization, oxygen masks would drop from the ceiling or pop out of the seat back in front of you. Masks drop automatically any time the internal cabin altitude climbs above 14,000 feet. If the automatic function does not operate properly, there is a flight-deck-controlled manual backup release. There is always one extra mask per row. Three seats would equal four masks just in case someone is holding a child in their lap.

Older planes utilize a gaseous oxygen system, meaning oxygen is stored in a large compressed air-type tank in the forward belly area of the plane. When your mask is pulled toward you, the flow of oxygen begins immediately. On a fully-loaded plane, there is enough oxygen to last twelve minutes.

Newer airplanes, in an effort to save weight, now use chemically generated oxygen. Located above every seat is a small oxygen generator. As the mask is pulled, a chemical reaction whose by-product is oxygen begins the oxygen flow immediately, though it can take up to twenty seconds to increase to full pressure. Again, assuming all masks are in use, there is about twelve minutes of oxygen.

Although twelve minutes of oxygen may seem like a paltry amount, in reality, an emergency descent necessitated by a cabin depressurization would only take two to three minutes, leaving ample reserve.

PORTABLE OXYGEN

There are small tanks of portable oxygen on board, designated for use by flight attendants who, in the event of an emergency, would be required to move around the cabin. These walkaround oxygen bottles double as emergency medical oxygen.

EMERGENCY EXITS

All the exits on an airplane have bright red exit lights located above them. Recently, though, the airlines and the FAA have realized that if a fire were to fill the plane with smoke, these signs might be difficult if not impossible to see. Older airplanes have been retrofitted, and newer airplanes are equipped with emergency path lighting, or track lighting, on the floor. These are a series of mostly white lights situated on the aisles of the floor, extending the length of the plane. The floor lights become red at or very near the exits. If the plane filled with smoke, passengers would be instructed to get as low as possible and crawl to the emergency exits. As a rule, heads should be kept no higher than the seat armrests. Passengers would then follow the white lights on the floor until they found the red lights. Then they'd make a ninety-degree turn and go out the door or emergency over-wing exits. Knowing the closest exit before an emergency is a safe habit to develop.

EMERGENCY ESCAPE SLIDES

On the narrow-body aircraft—including the MD-80, Boeing 737 and 727—the escape slides will open and fully inflate within three seconds. On the 757 it takes four seconds. Larger airplanes, like the 767 and 747, having larger slides because they are higher off the ground, require about five seconds.

If a slide fails to inflate automatically, there is a manual backup activated by pulling a well-labeled lanyard.

The slides on new airplanes also double as rafts for emergency ditchings. The older planes used to store their rafts in the ceiling, but as rafts became larger and heavier, carrying a raft to the emergency exit became more difficult. Within these rafts are survival kits, including such items as bailing buckets, an emergency inflation pump, a signal mirror, a canopy to protect from the sun, signaling flares, first-aid kits, flashlights, a sea anchor to slow the drift of the raft, a survival manual, seasickness pills, a whistle, drinking water, and even candy snacks.

LIFE PRESERVERS

For all extended flights over water, like the Gulf of Mexico, the Great Lakes, or the oceans, there must be flotation equipment on board. Besides the rafts that have already been mentioned, every seat has its own life preserver. They are located beneath the seat. You can double-check that it's there by feeling underneath the seat. They are checked regularly. Passenger life preservers are yellow; crew members wear orange.

They are inflated by pulling a lanyard, which triggers a compressed air cylinder. If that failed to work, there are manual inflation tubes to blow into. A tiny water-activated light that illuminates automatically is attached to the life preserver's shoulder. The light will work for eight to ten hours.

CHAPTER 5

COCKPIT PREPARATION AND AIRCRAFT SYSTEMS

As everyone knows, an airplane is an extremely complex vehicle. A Boeing 747 has about 4½ million parts, necessitating a parts catalog of 12,000 pages. Just to build a 747 requires over 100 miles of wire.

The cockpit, also referred to as the flight deck, is the central nervous system of the entire operation. There are more than 500 switches, dials, knobs, gauges, buttons, lights, and circuit breakers. The flight crew is required to know the function of every single one. The newer airplanes have up to 140 on-board computers, some accessed by the flight crew through two central flight-management computers, and some fully automatic.

In front of both the captain and co-pilot are a complete set of flight controls and flight instruments, so that either pilot can fly the airplane. Between the pilots is the radio equipment used to talk with Air Traffic Control, other aircraft, and the company. There is also new data-link communications equipment called Automatic Crew Addressing and Reporting System (ACARS), which is capable of faxing information between the ground and the aircraft and vice versa. Just forward of the radio console is the throttle quadrant, the location of the thrust levers, slats and flap controls, and speed brake handle. On the forward instrument panel, clearly visible to both pilots, are all the engine instruments and the weather radar display. The only prominent handle on the forward panel is the gear lever, used to raise and lower the landing gear, which is conspicuously away from all the other flight controls. On most aircraft, above that is the autopilot mode control panel—within easy reach of either pilot. Overhead on a two-pilot airplane are the controls for the basic systems, including fuel, electrical hydraulic, ice and rain protection, and pressurization. On a three-pilot airplane these controls are on a side facing the flight engineer's panel.

COCKPIT PREPARATION

After stowing their luggage, the first task the crew members do upon entering the cockpit is check the maintenance log book. The log chronicles the aircraft's most recent mechanical history. If the mechanic found the plane in satisfactory condition, he will sign the aircraft off as airworthy. If there was a problem and he has already fixed it, the log will indicate the problem, the repair, and his signoff. If the mechanic is still working on the plane, a red out-of-service tag is prominently displayed in the cockpit, indicating to the flight crew not to activate any switches.

REPAIRS

What if there is something wrong with the airplane that can't be fixed during the scheduled ground time between flights? In other words, if the plane is not completely 100 percent, can it still be airworthy? The answer is found in the MEL-CDL, an acronym for Minimum Equipment List and Configuration Deviation List. This on-board FAA-approved Aircraft Restrictions Manual clearly defines the acceptable parameters for less than a 100 percent perfect airplane.

Do not confuse the word *safe* for the word *perfect.* Take your car as an example. If the headlights on your car were faulty, your automobile would still be safe to drive during the daytime, even though your car is not perfect. Similar parameters work for an airplane also.

There are two types of mechanical problems covered by the MEL-CDL. First there are those things described as "no-go items," which are obviously required to be in perfect working order for every flight. For example, the wings, flight controls, engines, hydraulic system, landing gear, and tires. If they are not in perfect condition before departure, the airplane doesn't go until they are.

In order to minimize any chance of misinterpretation, the MEL is written as a "discrepancies you can fly safely with" manual. This means any maintenance item not specifically covered by the MEL, for whatever reason, automatically becomes a no-go item.

Then there are the systems not required on every flight. The MEL very specifically breaks down these problems into three distinct categories: (1) the flight is permitted back to a maintenance station where mechanics and parts are available to fix the problem; (2) maintenance can be deferred up to 72 hours; and (3) maintenance can be deferred up to ten days. In all three cases the applicable flight limitations must be observed. For example, if the wing anti-ice system is inoperative, you cannot fly into known icing conditions. If the oxygen masks are faulty in a row of seats, that row must be blocked off from passenger use.

There is a reason repairs are not always made immediately—the prohibitive cost of stocking every spare part for every single airplane at every airport in the country. All airlines stock essentials like tires, brakes, radios, and the other obvious no-go items, despite the huge cost. But not every station can store equipment such as air data computers, engine generators, and autopilots, especially equipment that rarely breaks down.

If an airplane has an item that cannot be immediately

fixed, it is entered into the aircraft log book as a "maintenance carryover item," or MCO. The on-board Aircraft Restrictions Manual will state the specific limitations for the flight, and as a secondary reminder to the flight crew, a placard fixed to the instrument panel acts as an advisory.

The CDL covers those items not necessary for flight. Cabin curtains, coffee makers, entertainment systems, access doors, and other cosmetic features. Repairs on these pieces of equipment are made in a timely manner and do not restrict the airworthiness of the plane.

Just like the exterior walkaround before each flight, the new crew must do an acceptance check of the cockpit to verify all the systems are normal.

THE ELECTRICAL SYSTEM

With more than 15,000 electronic devices on board an airplane, this system is obviously intricate and complex. There are three basic ways that planes receive electrical power.

The first is external power. When looking at the nose of an aircraft parked at the gate, you may have noticed a long extension-type cord connected to it. This usually runs from the jetway and is plugged into the nose area of the plane. Like a household appliance, external electrical power connects the plane with the local power company, which is more cost effective than having the airplane generate its own power.

Most aircraft use 120 volts A.C., just like your home, except the frequency at 400 Hertz (cycles per second) is far greater than your 60 cycles at home. Unlike your toaster oven, or refrigerator, aircraft systems are very sensitive to voltage and frequency fluctuations. If you have ever been sitting inside a plane at the gate and noticed the main lights go out and the emergency lights come on, it may have been caused by the external power temporarily surging out of tolerance, causing the airplane's electrical system—loaded with microchips and computers—to drop off line as protection. Resetting the system, just like resetting a circuit breaker at home, will correct a transient fault.

The second source of ground power comes from the APU—Auxiliary Power Unit. The APU is a small jet engine, about the size of an engine on a commuter-type aircraft (minus the propeller). It's housed internally near the tail of the plane. APU's are quite noisy, and more expensive than external power because of the added fuel usage. But they have the advantage of generating electrical power to very exact tolerances, while also generating the compressed air necessary to run the air-conditioning system on the ground.

The third form of electricity is the ship's generators, which are mounted to the plane's engines. A twin-engine airplane, like the 757 and 767, for example, have two engine-driven generators. As the engine rotates, it turns the generator, which creates electricity. Since engine speed is varied from takeoff to cruise to landing, the generator is connected to the engine through a CSD, a constant speed drive, which is a transmission-type device that keeps the generator speed constant through various flight regimes.

Each generator is capable of producing 90,000 watts, the equivalent of 750 amps. By comparison, your average household uses a maximum of 150 to 200 amps. As a backup to a double failure on a two-engine airplane, triple or quadruple failure on a three- or four-engine craft, the APU is started and can generate enough electrical power to operate the entire essential electrical system without interruption.

What if all the generators failed? And the APU? Then there is still a battery backup. The battery, which is constantly being charged by an on-board battery charger, stores enough power to run the essential electrical system for up to 30 to 45 minutes—more than ample time to fly to a suitable airport and land. On long overseas flights where you are more than 30 to 45 minutes from the closest airport, an additional electrical system is available. The

Hydraulic Motor Generator (HMG) uses circulating hydraulic fluid to turn an additional electric generator to provide power.

AIR-CONDITIONING AND PRESSURIZATION

These two systems are related, since the same air used to pressurize the airplane is also used to regulate temperature.

The pressurization system keeps the pressure of the air in the cabin as close to sea-level pressure as possible. Keep in mind: the percent of oxygen in the upper atmosphere is identical to the percent near the earth's surface, only the pressure of the air decreases. As an aircraft climbs, a mechanism to compress the air is needed. Interestingly, just as we need the relatively dense air of the lower atmosphere to breathe, those big engines need lots of dense air to mix with fuel to create the combustion that generates thrust. Thus the two requirements for sea level–type air can be met with one solution.

The first two sections of a modern turbofan engine, well in front of the parts of the engine associated with combustion, are simply air compressors. As air enters the big, wide intake of the front of the engine, it passes through thirteen stages of rotors, each compressing the outside air one step closer to sea-level density. At the end of the thirteenth stage we still have clean, healthy, breathable air, except the by-product of compression is heat. Even before the air reaches the multiple combustion chambers, the temperature of the air can reach up to 350 degrees.

This hot compressed air can be used in a number of ways. Primarily it flows into the second section of the engine to provide the air needed for combustion. But by opening up a series of bleed air valves, called such because they bleed air away from the engine, hot air can be routed to the parts of the aircraft that need anti-ice protection. Also, compressed air can be routed to the cabin to provide air at a breathable pressure.

Obviously, though, before this hot air is routed to the

cabin it needs to be sufficiently cooled to a more livable temperature. For just this reason the system is called the air-conditioning and pressurization system and not air-conditioning, heating, and pressurization.

The hot air then goes to two or three air-conditioning units called Air Cycle Machines. The capacity and number of units is dependent on the size of the airplane. The Air Cycle Machine serves the same function as your home air conditioner, converting hot air into cold air, but is different because it doesn't use freon or any other gases to cool the air.

Inside the ACM the hot bleed air is ducted—like the ducting in your house, except with protective thermal insulation—to the heat exchanger. Taking advantage of the cold outside temperature at cruising altitudes—down to −56 degrees—this cold air is scooped up through an intake near the front underbelly of the plane, allowed to pass around the airtight plumbing carrying the air, which dissipates the heat as the cold air is exhausted overboard. Multiple trips through the heat exchangers will cool this breathable air quickly. At lower altitudes and on the ground fans can be utilized to enhance the system.

Before exiting the Air Cycle Machine, the air is re-expanded for one additional stage of cooling. Simple physics says that compressed air will heat up and expanded air will cool down. In order to obtain the desired cabin temperature, air from three different sections of the ACM, hot, cool, and cold are mixed.

If an ACM temperature controller were ever to become erratic, causing fluctuating temperatures in the aircraft, a secondary manual backup can be used to move the temperature mixing valves. If the valves were to fail in the hot position, there are multiple automatic shutoff systems to force the system to put out colder air, or if necessary, turn that one ACM off completely. Since the flight attendants and pilots feel the same temperature of air as the passengers, the system rarely reaches a temperature causing an automatic trip-off.

Planes are divided into different independent temperature zones. Because humans give off heat, a section of the aircraft that is full requires more cooling than a section that is empty. The cockpit has its own zone because the heat generated by all the avionics and other instruments makes the demand for colder air greater than the rest of the plane. Since we all like slightly different temperatures, there is a tiny air-conditioning outlet above each and every seat, an individual valve that gets air from the cold side of the ACM. It is circulated by the aircraft gasper fan.

One additional point: Sometimes during the hot summer months, airplanes are too hot on the ground, and just after departure they become too cold. On the ground the Air Cycle Machines cannot work to capacity because the volume of air provided by the APU is significantly less than the engine compressors. After takeoff, they sometimes work too well, until they can be adjusted by the flight crew. Occasionally, then, on a hot day, condensation drips from the panels in the ceiling. Passengers naturally assume the plane is leaking, but what is really happening is the cold air plumbing is sweating, and the moisture droplets are dripping from the exterior part of the pipes. It's the same thing that occurs when a can of soda is taken from the refrigerator and placed on a counter; it sweats even if the can has never been opened. Under some temperature differences, fog can form and be mistaken for smoke. If there are extreme temperature differences between the cabin and the colder air-conditioning ducting, condensation can actually freeze and a little snow can fall.

PRESSURIZATION

The pressurization system on board an aircraft is one of the simpler systems to understand. The amount of air entering the cabin, after being cooled to the desired temperature, is nearly constant. By regulating the amount of air exiting the cabin, you can regulate the pressure inside.

Air enters continually at nearly 6000 cubic feet a minute. It takes only 180 seconds for the cabin to have a completely new supply of air. The amount exiting is determined by the position of an outflow valve. All aircraft have one or more large (one to two feet across) holes, usually near the tail of the plane, that can be regulated from fully opened to fully closed by moving an outflow valve. Fully open, all 6000 cubic feet of air will pass through the cabin and exit through the open outflow valve, keeping the plane completely unpressurized. Fully closed, the pressure will build to a point of maximum pressurization, and the automatic pressurization valves will open, returning the pressure to normal. Most of the time the multiple valves are regulated somewhere between fully open and fully closed, in extremely small increments to keep the internal pressure as desired. In the very unlikely case a small pressure leak were to develop around a door seal, for instance, the pressurization would be unaffected because the outflow valve would close farther, keeping the exiting air a constant.

Sometimes pressure changes can be felt in your ears. The pressurization rates of change are kept below 500 feet per minute while climbing and 300 feet per minute while descending. These are lesser rates than many of today's high-rise elevators. Surges are sometimes felt because the pressure-regulating valves that keep the inflow a constant volume do not adjust rapidly enough to the changing power settings of the engine.

The pressurization system has multiple redundant backups. All aircraft have a minimum of one fully automatic system, a standby automatic system, and a manual system where the pilots can control the outflow valve directly.

HYDRAULIC SYSTEM

An airplane hydraulic system is similar to the power steering or brakes in an automobile. It reduces the force necessary to operate the flight controls.

Multiple hydraulic pumps pressurize the system to 3000 psi (pounds per square inch). When the controls are moved in the cockpit, signals are sent via cables and/or wires to the hydraulic valves. As the valves are moved, the hydraulic fluid, a basically incompressible liquid, is forced from one part of the system to the actuators, the mechanisms that actually move the massive flight controls. Other components tied to the hydraulic system are: the landing gear and brakes; slats and flaps; speed brake/spoiler; and the nosewheel steering used on the ground.

Aircraft have at least three independent hydraulic systems, with a minimum of two pumps in each system. One system alone is capable of running all the essential hydraulic equipment. The pumps all have independent power sources, some engine-driven, some electric, and others driven by engine bleed air.

In the event all three independent systems were to fail simultaneously, there is a Ram Air Turbine (RAT) backup. On newer aircraft this turbine automatically drops from the lower fuselage, exposing a large propeller blade to the stream of air passing the plane. The propeller spins, turning a motor that pressurizes a standby hydraulic system. If the RAT fails to deploy automatically, the pilots have a manual override.

FUEL SYSTEM

As mentioned in a previous chapter, aircraft have what are called wet wings, meaning fuel is housed in the wings themselves. If additional fuel is required, it is stored in a center tank in the lower fuselage. However, it is more desirable to use the wing tanks first, because fuel in the wings adds to their structure and strength.

Refueling of all the tanks is accomplished from one location, usually at the leading edge of either wing. Fuel is pumped under pressure at a rate of 750 gallons per minute. Additional fueling hoses can be connected to increase the rate, a necessity when 25,000 to 50,000 gallons of fuel must be boarded for many of the long overseas flights.

A carryover from the propeller days, jets still have the overwing fueling caps, whereby a fueler can climb on the top of the wing and manually refill the plane.

There are multiple ways to determine exactly how much fuel is left in the tanks at any given time. Before the plane ever leaves the gate, the aircraft fueler must deliver to the pilots a copy of the fuel slip indicating exactly how much fuel was boarded at this station and the total quantity reading of his remote gauges. This information is compared with both the fuel totalizer and the individual tank quantity gauges. If there is any discrepancy, the error must be located before the appropriate repair can be made.

Using what is called the drip-stick method, the actual quantity of fuel in each tank can be exactly determined. Multiple narrow tubes with a hole in the center are pulled down from various locations in the tanks. If the tank is full, moving the stick down ever so slightly will cause fuel to flow over the top of the stick and out the tube. If the tank is completely empty, no fuel will drip even when the stick is drawn fully out. The calibrated drip stick will indicate directly the quantity of fuel in that tank.

Once the engines are started, the fuel used indicators become active. There are gauges that measure precisely the amount of fuel used by each individual engine. At pushback the crew knows exactly how much fuel they have on board. In the unlikely happenstance the entire fuel quantity system was to fail at once, they could still subtract the fuel used from the beginning total and ascertain the fuel remaining.

Each fuel tank has a minimum of two independent fuel pumps, each capable of pumping fuel under pressure to the engines. If both failed in the same tank, the engines still have the capability of suction feeding fuel from the tank to the engines. Additionally, they can also cross-feed fuel, or route fuel from the right tank to the left engine and vice versa.

CARGO HEATING SYSTEM

The cargo compartment is normally kept at a temperature around 45 degrees. If there are any live animals, a vent is opened to divert part of the pressurization and air-conditioning air, heating this section of the cargo compartment to a more comfortable 65 degrees. This vent switch is occasionally referred to as the dead dog switch, because an error in its operation can cause an animal to freeze, particularly on a long flight. However, it is becoming routine to wire this switch permanently in the on position. But not every airplane has been modified.

The reason for the cargo vent switch is that by reducing the air pressure and heat in the cargo compartment, you reduce the chance of something flammable that's been illegally carried in a passengers' luggage from catching on fire. Today's aircraft have heat and fire detectors, and fire extinguishers for the cargo compartment that can be remotely operated from the cockpit.

FLIGHT INSTRUMENTS

The basic flight instruments are grouped in the same position on every aircraft, which makes the transition from one aircraft to another easier. There are two types of flight instruments: the old-style electromechanical, which uses electricity to work a mechanical device. This system is excellent, but with many moving parts, regular maintenance is required. The new systems use CRT's—or Cathode Ray Tubes—like computer monitors. They have no moving parts and are virtually maintenance free. When the picture tube wears out, you can simply replace it. Current airplanes have no less than six screens. If one monitor should fail in flight, its information can be displayed on another screen. These new displays are commonly referred to as glass cockpits.

FLYING IN THE CLOUDS

In front of both the captain and co-pilot are attitude indicators. This instrument is a gyroscope that spins extremely fast, 20,000 RPM's, which keep the instrument perpendicular to the earth regardless of whether the plane is climbing or descending, turning left or right. As an airplane banks, for example, the case of the instrument has to move the same degree as the plane itself, because they are physically attached. However, the interior gyroscope, supported by free-swinging gimbals, stays level with the horizon at all times. The difference between the two is displayed to the pilots as the plane's attitude. On older planes the attitude indicator is electromechanical. On newer aircraft they are laser (light) gyroscopes. No less than three gyroscopes are required, with one being powered directly by the battery in case of a total electrical failure. On the new aircraft with laser gyros, an additional old-style electromechanical backup is still carried.

DETERMINING DIRECTION

Airplanes have compasses, but their use is limited. If you have ever used a compass, either the kind with the rotating needles that point to magnetic north or the models with a free-swinging compass card, you know how movement caused the compass to swing. Reliable readings were difficult in anything but a steady state. Include the radio and magnetic interference of an airplane, and you see a more precise form of directional information is needed.

On planes, heading information is received from compasses remotely located in the wing tips. This location reduces the interference. Their information is transmitted to the heading indicators in the cockpit, which, like the attitude indicator, has a built-in gyroscope that spins at a very high velocity, making the compass display immune to the motion of the plane.

Each pilot has a minimum of two heading indicators at his position. The captain's primary indicator serves as the co-pilot's secondary and vice versa, so a constant comparison can be made easily. If any inconsistencies exist between the independent systems, an instrument comparator warning will serve as a backup alert to the crew.

As is the case with attitude indicators, newer aircraft have replaced the electromechanical heading indicators with laser gyros. Since laser gyros operate at the speed of light, (186,000 miles per second), and are unaffected by interference, their accuracy is unsurpassed. In fact the same laser gyros used today were used on the Apollo Space Missions to the moon.

DETERMINING ALTITUDE

Altitude is determined by an altimeter, and two distinct types are installed on commercial aircraft. The first, the barometric altimeter, senses barometric pressure and converts that into a reading of height above sea level. As the plane ascends, the barometric pressures decrease, so the indicator senses less pressure. Barometric altimeters display altitude to the nearest 20 feet.

Because baro altimeters sense altitude above sea level, they will not read zero when you are on the ground. The lowest commercial airport in the United States is New Orleans at 4 feet above sea level. If you were on the ground at Denver, your barometric altimeter would read 5333 feet, the height above sea level at Stapleton Airport.

All cruising altitudes are assigned on the basis of feet above mean sea level or MSL. Mean sea-level altimetry is the most reliable over the entire flight regime, from takeoff to cruising altitude upward of 40,000 feet. Furthermore, all obstructions, including mountains, tall buildings, high antennas are displayed on aeronautical charts as height above sea level.

Every plane has two independent barometric altimeter systems, with an auxiliary backup for the captain and co-pilot.

The second altimeter system is the radio altimeter. By sending signals from the plane to the ground and measuring the time necessary for the signal to return, the exact height in feet above ground level (AGL) can be determined. Radio altimeters are used from the ground up to 2500 feet AGL. Above that their use would be limited. Radio altimeters on older aircraft are accurate to 10 feet; the latest equipment reads in 2-foot increments.

These two systems complement each other, especially on the approach to land. Airplanes approved for approaches and landings in foggy conditions where the runway visibility is poor must have a minimum of two independent radio altimeter systems to precisely measure the height above the runway during the last few moments prior to touchdown.

VERTICAL SPEED

Both barometric and radio altimeters give an accurate picture of current altitude, but do not directly measure the rate of change. When climbing or descending, it is important to be able to predict, with accuracy, your future altitude after a period of time. The vertical speed indicator, or VSI, is a barometric altimeter that measures the airplane's rate of change up or down in units of feet per minute. The VSI scale has a range from zero to plus or minus 6000 feet per minute, and is accurate to the nearest 100 feet.

How do you use it? Let us say you are cruising at 35,000 feet and wish to descend to 10,000 feet in exactly 25 minutes. By lowering the nose of the aircraft until the vertical speed indicator reads minus 1000 feet per minute rate of change, you would be level at 10,000 feet in the allotted time.

AIRSPEED

In front of both the pilot and co-pilot is an airspeed indicator similar to a car's speedometer. Its operation is much different, though. Basically, speed is determined by comparing two different readings.

In the front of the plane there are several pitot tubes protruding from the nose. During the walkaround they are checked to be free and clear. As the plane flies, air is forced into these tubes. As the forward velocity is increased, the air pressure, the ram air into these tubes, also increases.

Also, on the side of the fuselage are static ports, little holes strategically located where the air is relatively still even in flight. By comparing the ram air to the still air, airspeed is determined.

As a carryover possibly from the seafaring days, all airspeed is displayed in nautical miles per hour, commonly called knots. Since a nautical mile is 15 percent greater than a conventional road map statute mile, a knot of airspeed is 15 percent greater than miles per hour.

Unlike a car speedometer, the basic airspeed indicator doesn't indicate true speed throughout the entire flight regime. The system, which begins registering at 60 knots (69 mph), depends on air being rammed into the pitot tubes. As an airplane climbs, the air density decreases, so less molecules are available to the airspeed system.

The difference between the plane's true airspeed and the indicated airspeed read on the cockpit gauge become more apparent the higher you climb. For example, at 10,000 feet if your airspeed indicator reads 300 knots (345 mph), that would be very close to your true airspeed. However, at 35,000 feet your airspeed gauge may only indicate 260 knots (299 mph), even though you are really cruising at 460 knots (529 mph), because the pressure of the molecules available to be rammed into the pitot tube is significantly reduced.

The next question might very well be, with all those fancy computers on board, why can't the airspeed gauge be recalibrated? The answer is, you don't want it to be. Indicated airspeed, by its very definition of indicating the molecules available to the pitot tubes—and thus molecules available to support the wings, which support the rest of the plane in flight—is the truest measure of aircraft performance.

However, Air Traffic Control, whose primary responsibility is traffic separation, is not interested in performance airspeed, but the actual true airspeed. At the higher altitudes airspeed is measured in Mach numbers because they are more accurate. You may have heard the term Mach as it relates to supersonic air travel. Planes that are capable of flying faster than the speed of sound (760 miles per hour at sea level) are traveling faster than Mach 1. Commercial airliners are built to cruise at the more economical Mach .78–Mach .86, or 78–86 percent of the speed of sound.

GROUND SPEED

Ground speed is how fast the plane is traveling over the ground. If we are cruising at 500 knots with a 100-knot tailwind, our ground speed will be 600 knots. Make a 180 degree U-turn into the wind and your ground speed will drop to 400 knots, even though your true airspeed of 500 knots never changes.

The prevailing upper air winds in the United States go from west to east. You can see why a Los Angeles–to–New York flight takes less time than New York to L.A.

TAXI SPEED

The cockpits of tall, widebody aircraft like the 767, L-1011, DC-10, 747, A-300, are so high off the ground that taxi speed indicators are needed to accurately judge speed —especially when turning a corner on a taxiway. Since the normal airspeed indicator does not register until 60 knots, a separate taxi speed indicator that senses tire rotation just like in your automobile is provided for speeds from zero to 25 knots.

LOCAL WEATHER

After the cockpit crew is satisfied that all the systems are in perfect working order, the local weather is checked on an ATIS frequency. ATIS stands for Automatic Terminal Information Service, and is a continuous loop tape recording of the most current local weather, field conditions, and status of general gate-holds. It is a time-saving device for the Air Traffic Controllers, who instead of having to read the weather, simply verify it has been received. Each new ATIS tape has the time of recording and a letter code to indicate it is current.

AIR TRAFFIC CONTROL CLEARANCE

Within thirty minutes of departure, and not before, the pilots radio the ATC pre-taxi clearance frequency, commonly called clearance delivery, to receive the specific route clearance filed by dispatch. If ATC cannot grant you your requested routing, an amended clearance will be issued. If there are any ATC delays in effect, an EDC— Expect Departure Clearance time—will be given, assuming the length of the delay is known.

When issuing a clearance, ATC will verify the destination airport, assign a departure SID if appropriate, give an initial climb to altitude—a hold down altitude until routed away from the inbound flights—an expected cruising altitude, the departure radio frequency (the first ATC controller to call after takeoff), and a distinct transponder code (more on this later).

Airlines routinely transport donor organs used in transplant operations. There are times, especially when ATC delays are in effect, that a crew may wish to designate their flight as a Lifeguard Flight. By doing so, expedited handling and routing can be obtained, helping to ensure that the human organ shipments reach their destinations in the allotted time.

ACCEPTANCE CHECKLIST

Though at this point all preflight items have been checked and double-checked, verification of this fact is accomplished by using a written predeparture checklist, featuring more than 60 items. One crew member reads while the other pilot verifies that each and every switch, button, and control is in its correct position.

CHAPTER 6

BASIC AERODYNAMICS

The essence of any airplane flight, whether it is an old-fashioned propeller plane or a jumbo 747, boils down to four basic forces acting upon the aircraft—lift, weight, thrust, and drag. Lift is necessary to overcome the airplane's weight, and thrust is required to overcome the plane's drag.

THRUST

Quite simply, engines produce thrust, which provides the energy to go forward. A car engine, for example, creates forward momentum by producing thrust and transferring it through an axle to wheels. The wheels are turned to provide forward movement. Unlike a car, a plane uses the thrust from its powerful engines to create what's called a relative wind. The relative wind passes over and under the wings, creating lift.

RELATIVE WIND

If you are traveling 50 miles per hour in a car on a perfectly calm day in the desert, when there's absolutely no wind blowing, and then stick your hand out the window, you are going to feel a wind coming from the front of the car to the back, and blowing at 50 mph. The car has generated a relative wind that's moving at the same speed but in the opposite direction. It's the same with an airplane: Fly at 200 knots and there is an equal and opposite relative wind.

LIFT

Lift is the upward force created by the wings to keep the plane in the air. Everyone has probably generated lift on numerous occasions. If you've ever stuck your arm out the window of a car and then moved your hand around to let the wind blow across it at different angles, you've generated lift. Tilt your hand upward slightly and it will want to rise up. Down slightly, and it will be pushed in that direction. Now cup your hand just a bit so it's no longer flat. Feel the increase in force against your hand.

On an airplane, lift is generated in much the same way. A plane's wing is designed so that the top has a greater curve than its relatively flat underside. This affects the way in which it passes through the air. Picture, for example, two molecules of air both getting to the front, or leading, edge of the wing at the same time. One molecule is going to go above the wing, the other below it.

The molecule traveling on top, because of the curved surface, has to cover a greater distance. Yet both molecules are going to meet at the trailing edge of the wing at the same time—a property of nature—which means they are moving at two different speeds. The one on top must travel faster. By traveling at different speeds, the molecules create a low pressure area on the top side and a high pressure area on the bottom side. The result—lift. You just learned the basics of Bernoulli's Law and the effect of "Venturi" action. In simple terms, if you have forward movement, you have an equal and opposite relative wind; if you have relative wind, you have molecules passing over and under the wings. If you have molecules passing over and under the wings, you have lift. Since the wings are attached to the airplane, the whole thing is lifted. Interestingly, more lift is created by the low pressure on the top of the wing than the high pressure underneath.

WHAT AFFECTS LIFT?

Four factors come into play when talking about lift.

First is the angle of attack, which defines the angle between the relative wind and the wing. In a car, if you put your hand outside the window and hold it fairly level, there isn't too much force on it. The more you tilt it upward, the greater the amount of force pushing your hand up also. By changing this angle of attack you can increase and decrease the amount of lift generated. It's the same with an airplane's wings. However, every wing also has a maximum angle of attack, above which the lift capability decreases rapidly. Using the car analogy again, if you held your hand blunt against the wind, you'd only feel a pushing force and no lift. Military aircraft have so much excess thrust that they can generate a relative wind even when climbing straight up. The limits for airliners are less.

Second is the wing area, which is nothing more than the size of the wings. Most people assume that a tiny Cessna flies better than a large 747. But the important factor isn't the plane's weight. Rather, it's how much does each square foot of wing area have to lift.

Third is the air density. This is one of the reasons it requires a longer takeoff run on hot, humid days at high-elevation airports. The air is less dense, and as the air density decreases, the lift also decreases.

Fourth is the plane's speed. Returning again to the car analogy, if you put your hand out the window and increase the car's speed, you will generate more force on your hand and more potential lift. It's the same with an airplane. The higher the speed, the more lift generated. A little more physics—the amount of lift generated is the square of the velocity. Accelerating from 200 to 400 knots quadruples the lift.

WEIGHT

The simplest of the four basic forces acting on a plane, weight is the opposite of lift. If an airplane weighs 300,000 pounds on the ground, that's also how much it totals in the air; 300,000 pounds of lift must be generated to overcome the weight or downward gravitational pull of the plane.

DRAG

Drag is the opposite of thrust. There are two types of drag: (1) parasite drag, which is the drag of the plane itself, and (2) induced drag, which is the by-product of lift and is proportional to airspeed—increasing your speed increases your lift, but also increases the induced drag. Induced drag plus the parasite drag equals the total drag that has to be overcome to get forward velocity.

HOW DOES AN AIRPLANE FLY?

A plane needs lift to get off the ground. To generate lift, it's necessary to have forward velocity. Forward velocity will produce an equal and opposite relative wind, and the relative wind passing over and under the wings will, in turn, create lift.

Lift is generated when there is excess thrust. More thrust than drag is required in order to accelerate the airplane. If there is more thrust than drag, then there can be more lift than weight, and this makes it possible to climb.

When the plane is at cruise, it's neither accelerating nor decelerating, climbing nor descending. At cruise, the amount of thrust is equal to the amount of drag, and the amount of lift is equal to the amount of weight. It's in a steady state.

If less thrust than drag is generated, then the plane will slow down. When it slows, there is less air passing over and under the wings; the weight becomes greater than the lift. The result: the airplane will descend.

WHY THE PLANE WOULDN'T FALL IF THE ENGINES STOPPED

As long as there is relative wind moving over and under the wings, lift is generated. When the plane is either in level flight or climbing, the relative wind is maintained using engine thrust that provides the power to move us through the air straight and level, or uphill. But what if all the engines were to quit?

First, the aircraft's weight hasn't changed just because the engines quit. The plane still needs only to generate enough lift to overcome the weight. How is this done?

A car that losses its engines might try to coast downhill. A plane only has to lower its nose. If all the engines were to fail at once, the pilots would point the airplane downhill. Enough lift will be generated to keep the plane safely airborne until an engine is restarted. At 35,000 feet even a jumbo jet can glide for about 70 miles, simply by coasting. Remember, the glide ratio is a function of how much lift has to be generated by each square foot of wing, not the total size or weight.

In fact, on almost every flight there comes a point on

descent when the pilots will pull the power back to idle and let the plane glide. Gliding is a normal part of almost every flight.

FLAPS AND SLATS

Every wing is designed to have a perfect speed—remember that speed affects lift—at which it's most efficient. Air transport wings, for instance, are designed to fly at extremely high speeds, upward of 600 mph. But to achieve this type of efficiency, its low speed efficiency is sacrificed. This is where flaps and slats become important. If a commercial airliner didn't have flaps and slats, it would have to accelerate to about 170 knots in order to generate enough lift to fly. With flaps and slats, minimum flying speed is nearer 100 knots, though greater takeoff and landing speeds are used for safety.

What flaps and slats do is increase the size of the wings about 20 percent. They increase the curvature, which also increases the lift, and utilizing the various combinations, it's possible to increase the lift of the wing some 80 percent. Why not leave flaps and slats out all the time? Because they'd create drag, which would reduce cruising speeds and sacrifice efficiency. Most planes have a flap and slat structural speed limit of 250 to 280 knots, so they are used for takeoff and landing, allowing shorter takeoff rolls, slower approach speeds, and less required landing distance; less wear and tear on the landing gear, tires, and brakes; and better slow speed in-flight stability.

STALL

When a car engine quits, it's said to have stalled. In terms of airplanes, a stall is totally unrelated. It has nothing at all to do with the engines, but the aerodynamics of the wing itself. A stall means very little or no lift is being generated. Not enough relative wind is available. Either the speed is too low or the maximum angle of attack has been exceeded. If the plane is on the ground, the wing is essentially stalled. There's no lift.

If the flight crew attempted to climb too steeply while airborne, the wing could stall from an excessive angle of attack. It's as if you were holding your hand out a car window, palms blunt to the air. You still have forward speed, but there's not enough relative wind passing over and under the wing.

Airline pilots never, never, fly any slower than 30 percent above the minimum speed that the wing can fly, whether during takeoff, landing, or cruise. So there is a big margin for error. Let's examine the worst-case scenario. If by some chance the plane did get too slow, a warning system would alert the pilots they were within 5 percent of minimum speed for this flap and slat configuration. If you continued to slow and actually stalled the wing, a stall recovery would involve lowering your angle of attack. Either lower the nose of the aircraft or add power—remember, there's nothing wrong with the engines—or do both simultaneously. A full recovery can be made in seconds.

FLYING SLOW

Planes are designed so that when cruising near maximum airspeed, the aircraft will be flying level. Normally we cruise slightly slower than maximum speed for fuel economy. If the plane is flown slower, there's less air passing over and under the wings, which means less lift. To compensate, the nose is raised. Normal economy cruise requires a nose-up pitch of 1 to 3 degrees. Slowing down further means another increase in pitch if we wish to keep from descending. Eventually we will slow to the point where flaps and slats are needed. Extending them increases lift so the degree of nose-up pitch required is less and the nose of the aircraft can be lowered. As we maneuver for our approach to land, we will slow further. Again the pitch is increased to compensate. It is common to see aircraft landing with their nose pitched up 5 to 7 degrees—this is also a design feature, so on landing, the main landing gear in the back touch down on the runway first.

FLIGHT CONTROLS

There are three basic flight controls: the elevator, the ailerons, and the rudder. The elevator, as the name implies, controls the pitch or the climbs and the descents. The ailerons control the angle of bank, which determines the rate of turn. The rudder controls the yaw, which keeps the tail of the fuselage following the nose. The basic flight controls share the same aerodynamic principles as the wing itself. All of the simple explanations about relative wind and lift still apply.

The elevator, located horizontally on the tail of the aircraft, generates lift just like the wing. By moving the control column in the cockpit back and forward, the elevator moves up and down. When the tail climbs, the nose of the airplane must go down an equal and opposite direction, since they are securely bolted together. Pushing the control column forward makes the airplane descend. Climbing is exactly the opposite. Pull back on the control column and the tail loses lift and goes down. The loss of lift causes the tail to descend and the nose to rise.

A stabilizer just forward of the elevator is used to reduce the amount of work the elevator has to do. During a long climb, you would get tired if you had to maintain back pressure on the control column all the way to cruise altitude. With an actuator switch on the control column, the stabilizer can be moved up or down to infinite fixed positions. This is called trimming an airplane. Once the stabilizer is moved to the new position, the force required by the elevator is removed and the plane holds the new pitch attitude. The new pitch attitude will be maintained until another change is needed.

The ailerons are mounted on the trailing edge of the wing near the tips. If there's also a second set, they will be located about halfway between the wing root and the first set. An airplane is banked when it's turned, it leans left or right. Bicycles and boats are similar; they both lean when they turn. How steeply does an airplane bank? Pilots limit the bank angles to 25 to 30 degrees, even though the planes are capable of more than double that amount. In fact, in recurrent training, pilots regularly practice steep turns to keep those skills sharp.

The mechanics of a turn are simple. When the control column is turned, one set of ailerons on one side goes up, while the set on the other side goes down. The wings then develop a slightly different amount of lift. The side developing more goes up, the other side goes down. Moving the control column back the other way rolls the plane out of the bank. The speed brake panels located on the trailing edge of the top portion of the wing are used to augment the bank capability. When turning left, the speed brakes on the left side raise up slightly and automatically assist the ailerons. This is the only time the left and right speed brakes can be used independently.

The rudder is located on the vertical portion of the tail, and is controlled by foot pedals. Both pilots have a set of rudder pedals. The rudder controls the yaw of the airplane, which is the level left and right movement of the nose. The rudder is used only slightly in a turn—to offset the asymmetric drag on the wing created by a bank, not to actually turn the plane.

A fundamental reason for the rudder is to keep the airplane flying straight were an engine failure to occur. If the right engine failed and the left engine was flying at full power, there would be a tendency for the airplane to want to turn (yaw) right because of the asymmetric thrust. Stepping on the left rudder pedal would stop this motion. The rudder also enables landings in a crosswind. Let's say there was a strong wind from the right side during the landing. If the plane lined up straight for the runway, the wind would have a tendency to push the plane left, or "downstream," away from the runway centerline. Banking the airplane slightly into the wind will stop this drift, just like when crossing a flowing river you aim upstream to end up on the opposite bank. But by banking into the wind, the plane's nose will not be straight down the runway. Using the opposite rudder, the nose can be accurately aligned.

INHERENT STABILITY

When looking at an airplane from the terminal building, you can see that the wings are higher at the tip than the root. This upward angle of the wings is called dihedral. Dihedral gives an airplane a great deal of inherent stability. Lift is always generated exactly perpendicular to the wing surface. If the two wing surfaces are pointed slightly toward each other, the lift vectors (lines) will cross somewhere above the fuselage. The resulting stability is similar to the stability in your car. If you turn the steering wheel in your car and let go, the tendency is for the steering wheel to return to center, and the car will eventually straighten out. A plane has the same built-in stability.

G FORCES

There are occasional times in an airplane when you feel heavier than you really are. The normal g (gravitational force) is greater and presses you into your seat a little harder. This force is felt the most during a turn or a quick level-off or bumpy turbulence. For example, in a 30-degree bank turn, the g force is 1.15, 15 percent greater than the normal 1 g felt on earth. Pilot techniques can eliminate some of the g forces felt in flight, but not all of them.

The basic aerodynamic principles of flight are straightforward. No matter how advanced and complex an airliner becomes, the four basic forces—*lift* to overcome *weight* and *thrust* to overcome *drag*—remain unchanged.

CHAPTER 7

EMERGENCY WARNING SYSTEMS

There are always two or three pilots (depending on the type of plane) in the cockpit at all times, continuously scanning the instruments and gauges to check the airplane and its systems. Furthermore, pilots work as a team and double-check each other. However, the basic principle of aviation is safety, and one way to increase safety is to increase redundancy. This section concerns the myriad warning systems on board that provide the backups to the flight crew.

DARK COCKPIT

In the cockpit all lights, including individual system lights and warning alert lights, are designed using a dark cockpit concept. This means that if all systems are turned on and working normally, there are no lights visible. The only lights on during a normal flight are the few green lights, such as the green gear down and locked lights, indicating that system is functioning normally. Switch positions are uniformly designed also. If up is on for one switch, it's the same for all the switches. On newer aircraft using a push-button type switch, in is always on and out is off.

LIGHT BULBS

Every light on the airplane contains a minimum of two bulbs. If a light bulb burns out, there is a backup. If the backup were to burn out as well, it can be replaced with one from the complete set of replacement bulbs carried in the cockpit.

SYSTEM MONITORS

On some of the early jet aircraft, the third pilot was the system monitor. He alerted the captain and co-pilot if a warning light appeared on the flight engineer's panel. On newer aircraft, the advisories, cautions, and warnings are grouped together on annunciator panels and can be scanned at a glance. The annunciator panel, which in flight should be completely blank, highlights a specific abnormal, directing you to the appropriate system and its redundant amber light. Just in case the pilots did not see the annunciator panel light, or the system light, in front of them are glare shield master warning and caution lights.

The latest system, called EICAS—Engine Indicating and Crew Alert System—goes a step further. A dual computer monitor warning system, it detects malfunctions, displays the specific problem on a CRT (mini TV) screen and prioritizes the degree of urgency. Whereas the older systems had a light to indicate part of a system was not as it should be, the new EICAS system tells the pilots exactly what part. Furthermore, the computers are able to differentiate between malfunctions that can be fixed in the air and problems that require ground maintenance. If both of the two independent EICAS computers failed, there are still the basic alerts.

Alerts come in varying degrees of severity. A warning requires immediate corrective action, so is always indicated with a red light, plus a siren, bell, computer-generated voice, or beeper. Examples of warnings would be an engine fire, or rapid depressurization. On EICAS equipped airplanes, amber alert lights are divided into two categories: cautions and advisories. Cautions indicate some kind of system fault. Timely corrective action is required, but not necessarily urgently. Some cautions have aural warnings, but the less urgent ones do not. An example of a caution would be an engine overheat. Advisories are the least urgent. They usually indicate a component of a system has malfunctioned, but the system is still operating. Corrective action can be taken as time permits. An example of an advisory is a faulty air-conditioning valve, or an electrical problem that has already been isolated or bypassed by the automatic backups.

FIRE WARNING

Everyone is concerned about fires. Each engine, the APU, the wheel well areas (hot brakes), and the cargo compartments have fire detection and prevention systems. Engines are mounted on struts to put distance between them and the rest of the aircraft. Even tail engines are isolated and shielded. Each engine has overheat detection systems and multiple fire loop sensors. An overheat may require no more than retarding the power slightly to reduce the internal temperature. An engine fire is more involved.

Both fire loops—the sensors loop around the entire engine—must detect a fire before the fire bells, alarms, and red warning lights are triggered. This prevents an inadvertent engine shutdown due to one faulty fire loop. If only one system does go off, a fire test system checks each fire detection system and distinguishes the reliable from the faulty. If there's no reliable test of either fire alarm system, then you have to assume a fire and take the required corrective action.

TAKEOFF CONFIGURATION WARNING

Takeoff is obviously a critical part of any flight. As a double-check to the flight crew taxi checks and their verified completion on a written checklist, there are both a takeoff configuration warning horn and red warning lights. If any one of the essential takeoff components are improperly set, a horn will sound and red lights will flash. On some airlines this horn is tested on taxi-out each flight and can be heard in the cabin. Takeoff flaps and slats set, ground spoilers completely stowed, and the elevator stabilizer (for pitch control) in the takeoff range, must all be completed, or the horn will blare at initial power application.

LANDING CONFIGURATION WARNING

Like takeoff, specific parameters have to be met when a plane is landing. Obviously, the landing gear must be lowered prior to touchdown. But as a redundant check, there is a warning system that would aurally and visually warn the pilots were the gear not down and locked. The flaps and slats are also wired into the landing configuration warning system. Though a plane can be landed with partially extended flaps and slats, or even with them fully retracted, a warning is sounded if the flap/slat setting is unintentionally abnormal. The speed brakes are regularly used on an approach to descend and slow down at the same time. But because they increase the descent rate, they are never used flying close to the ground. When descending through approximately 800 feet AGL as measured by the radio altimeters, all three of the landing configuration warnings are active.

OVERSPEED WARNING

All airplanes, like your car, have maximum speeds. The maximum speed your automobile engine can accelerate your car up a hill or on level ground is well below the structural limits of the car body itself. However, take that same car and drive it at full throttle down a steep incline, and that car may be a little less stable. Airplanes are much the same during climb, cruise, and descent. A red line on the airspeed indicator, which varies with altitude, indicates the maximum, never-exceed speed. There are both a warning horn and red lights to prevent exceeding this limit. All the built-in protections against flutter, vibration, and general structural strength are based on speeds 25 percent above the never-exceed speed. So if the horn goes off at the airspeed red line, it is time to slow down before accelerating any closer to those critical limits. Slowing an airplane is a simple procedure. Retarding the power, deploying the speed brakes to increase the aerodynamic drag, or simply shallowing out the descent is all that is required.

CABIN ALTITUDE WARNING

Normally in cruise, the interior cabin altitude is kept at the 6000 to 7000 foot level. If the cabin pressure ever decreased, causing the cabin altitude to rise above 10,000 feet, a warning would sound. With a sudden change in cabin pressures, one possibly caused by a rapid depressurization, the pressure change felt in your ears, the gauges and the red lights would alert the crew. If it didn't, then the horn would alert them to don their oxygen masks until the cabin pressure could be controlled. Above 14,000 feet cabin altitude, supplemental oxygen becomes available to the passengers from the automatically deployed overhead masks. When the system is restored or the plane descends to a breathable altitude, supplemental oxygen is no longer needed. Slow leaks do not cause pressurization problems because the outflow valve is able to compensate for the leak by closing slightly more than normal.

STALL WARNING

As noted earlier, though called a stall warning, it has nothing to do with the engines. It's a term often misunderstood, having to do with the performance of the wings. A commercial airline, which can fly with all the engines shut down like a glider, could stall with full power if it tried to climb straight up. As discussed in the basic aerodynamics, a plane stalls when not enough air is passing over and under the wings, resulting in insufficient lift. An airplane's stall speed varies with flap and slat configuration, weight, altitude, and angle of bank. Below the stall speed, an airplane will not fly. Pilots never fly anywhere close to this minimum speed. All airspeeds for slow speed flight during takeoff and landing are calculated on a minimum margin of safety of 30 percent or greater. If the plane inadvertently slowed to within 5 percent of the stall speed, lights and horns alert the pilots before the stall occurs. A "stickshaker" will even vibrate the control column to further warn you. If, by freak chance, the warnings were ignored and the plane stalled, full recovery could be made almost instantaneously by increasing the airspeed with power or lowering the pitch angle, or both. Stall recognition and stall recovery are studied and practiced at the required pilot recurrent training every six months.

GROUND PROXIMITY WARNING (GPWS)

The Ground Proximity Warning System is really a multiple warning system in one. Tied to the radio altimeters, the system is only active within 2500 feet of the ground. Four conditions will activate the warning that includes lights and a computer-generated voice alert: a descent immediately after takeoff, flying into rapidly rising terrain, excessive descent rates, and getting too low on the electronic glide slope on the approach to land.

WINDSHEAR WARNING

Windshear alert systems are currently being installed on new aircraft and retrofitted on planes already in service. Windshear, a common but little understood term, involves a very extreme change in the wind direction and velocity over a very short distance. Hence the name shear. Certain known conditions give rise to a possible windshear—such as nearby thunderstorm activity—and are avoided. In cruise, windshear causes turbulence but no other great hazard. Near the ground, the temporary decrease in lift caused by a very severe shear must be overcome. On approach, pilots are trained to begin windshear recovery techniques if any of the following occurs: the airspeed unexpectedly fluctuates plus or minus 15 knots, the vertical speed increases or decreases 500 feet per minute for no apparent reason, or if it is taking unusual pitch or power to fly the approach. Though the criteria is very specific, multiple red warning lights—one located right on the attitude indicator directly in front of each pilot—and a computer-generated voice stating "Windshear, Windshear," will alarm to further alert the pilots to initiate the safety procedures. Full power and the maximum rate of climb will be used to fly away from the shear.

AUTOPILOT DISCONNECT WARNING

If the autopilot isn't working properly or disconnects, red warning lights and horns sound. In cruise only one autopilot is employed. If the disconnect was for a faulty autopilot, another one can be engaged. Most airliners are equipped with at least two, many with three. If the disconnect was intentional, the alerts act as a confirmation that the disconnect was complete even though it is easily felt in the flight control yoke. Since the autopilot is capable of trimming the airplane to an inherently stable flight condition—if you are climbing, it trims for a steady rate of climb; straight and level, it trims to remain in steady cruise—an unintentional disconnect may not cause a change in the flight attitude. Without a warning or light, the disconnect could go unnoticed for a few seconds or so.

When flying on autopilot in cruise, holding the flight control wheel is not necessary. During an autopilot approach, the rules change. The pilot operating the autopilot will also keep his hand on the control wheel in order to sense an unintentional disconnect immediately and be in a position to take over manually.

AUTOTHROTTLE DISCONNECT CAUTION

Just like the autopilot disconnect, if autothrottles are installed, there will be a disconnect alert. Whether or not the throttles are intentionally or unintentionally disconnected, the caution beeper and lights will alarm. A second push of the disconnect button will silence the beeper.

SPEED BRAKE EXTENDED WARNING

Speed brakes (spoilers on the ground), the large panels on the top of the wings, create a significant amount of drag when raised from their flush position. This is precisely what they are designed to do. However, there are certain times during flight, specifically takeoff, initial climb, and on the final approach to land, that their deployment would be inopportune. There is sufficient power to overcome their added drag, but a speed brake extended warning below 800 feet alerts the flight crew to the extra drag and the higher than normal descent rate that will be the result. Some airplanes do not allow the speed brakes to be used with the flaps and slats extended more than a certain amount, regardless of altitude.

FUEL CAUTION

Not surprisingly, some passengers express concern about the aircraft running low or even out of fuel. The amount of fuel carried on each flight far exceeds the amount required, and that amount is verified to be in the fuel tanks with double- and triple-checks. Extra fuel is boarded for all known and unanticipated delays. Extra fuel is also boarded in case the headwinds are stronger than forecast. Pilots, dispatchers, and fuelers are a conservative, cautious group by nature. Still, low-fuel warning lights are installed. The fuel burn per engine per hour is different for each type of airplane, but when the fuel quantity gets down to where there is only 40 to 50 minutes' worth left, the low-fuel lights will indicate it is time to land. Most pilots have never seen this light outside of practice simulators.

ALTITUDE DEVIATION CAUTION

All commercial airliners have altitude alert systems. When Air Traffic Control clears you to a new altitude, whether climbing or descending, the new clearance altitude is entered into the alert window. When approaching the clearance limit altitude, an altitude light and beeper serve as a reminder. Once steady at that altitude, any deviation of more than 250 feet will also cause the alert.

TRAFFIC ALERT AND COLLISION AVOIDANCE

Collision avoidance is one of the primary reasons for Air Traffic Control. Even if a pilot were constantly looking out the window, the incredible airspeed of the modern jets makes seeing other planes and then avoiding them an inefficient safeguard. ATC keeps all planes separated by lesser amounts near the airport, where the speeds are slower and when the pilots can see the other planes, and greater amounts at the higher altitudes and faster speeds. ATC does a fantastic job. Pilots would not fly if they did not completely trust the Air Traffic Controllers and their ground-based radar equipment.

The ATC computers are programmed for collision avoidance. If two aircraft were to get too close, within 2000 feet vertically and 10 miles laterally at the higher cruise altitudes, a conflict alert would signal the controller and he would ask one of the planes to turn or change altitudes. As an added safeguard the FAA has mandated, no later than the end of 1993, a Traffic Alert and Collision Avoidance System (TCAS) be installed on all commercial airplanes.

All airliners have transponders with encoding altimeters. When a distinct four-digit code is entered into them, they send the plane's exact location and altitude to ATC. ATC uses this transponder information to track all the flights. With TCAS, the individual planes will be able to receive and interpret the transponder information from other nearby aircraft just like ATC. If two aircraft are converging, the two TCAS systems can "talk" with each other and alert both crews which way to turn to avoid a collision. This by no means is a substitute for ATC, but it does act as an additional safeguard, and has significant promise.

MISCELLANEOUS CAUTIONS AND ADVISORIES

There are numerous other cautions and advisories, because each and every system has some kind of alert to notify the flight crew of any small problem before it becomes something bigger. But as we have continually stressed, they are cautions and advisories, since a component failure may not render a system inoperative. If it does, there are multiple redundant systems and emergency backups for the backups. For instance: flaps that do not extend hydraulically can be lowered electrically. If the electric system does not work, you simply land with the flaps up. The loss of electrical power from an engine generator can be replaced with power from another engine generator, or the APU generator, or the standby battery. A fuel pump failure is not a problem, another fuel pump will do the job. If the automatic pressurization system is working erratically, it can be substituted with another system that is good or with the manual backup. For the most part, though, things just don't break.

What we should conclude from this chapter is that an airplane is designed to be user friendly. Using horns, buzzers, lights, and even computer-generated voices, the plane can talk to the flight crew. Pilots are thoroughly trained and retrained semiannually, continuously checked and rechecked. Though pilots individually and as a team are expected to be perfect and correct in every decision 100 percent of the time, installing these myriad emergency warning systems is an inexpensive insurance policy. Except for the routine warnings like the autopilot disconnect, the other warnings are heard only in the aircraft simulator during practice. Still, if they are only needed one time, they are a welcome added safety feature.

CHAPTER 8

MAINTENANCE

Airplane maintenance is vastly different than the maintenance on your car. Aircraft are maintained on an exact preventive maintenance schedule, meaning the components of the plane are replaced or overhauled long before any problem develops. All maintenance is done by FAA-licensed mechanics, and the record of their work, date, and their certificate number are all permanently recorded in the aircraft log. Major airlines spend close to two million dollars a day on this progressive maintenance program that keeps even the older aircraft in mint condition.

MAINTENANCE HISTORY

Aircraft manufacturers certify all the individual parts of an airplane for a useful life of a specific number of cycles and/or hours of service. Aircraft cycles are the number of flights the airplane has made; hours of service is the total flight time. Short-haul aircraft may fly eight flights a day accumulating 12 hours in service. A long-haul widebody aircraft can fly 12 hours in just one flight. Both parameters are needed to define the limits of the individual aircraft components, because cycles cause more wear and tear than actual hours. To arrive at these "to be overhauled" or "to be replaced" limits, the manufacturers test the critical parts individually, even sacrificing one entire airplane to a total stress-to-destruction test so the strength of the plane can be accurately analyzed. Airplanes have been tested to the equivalent of thirty years in service and 100,000 cycles with no critical failures.

Once a plane enters service, the airlines become legally responsible to maintain that plane to exacting standards, and document in a permanent record its maintenance history. Each individual part on each individual airplane has its own unique number and reliability record. Each part can be tracked by computer, so its exact number of cycles and/or hours can be recorded.

The maintenance history of an airplane develops with each flight. Flight crews are responsible for completing an aircraft log for every flight. Nearly 100 percent of the time no entry is made, signifying every component of the aircraft worked perfectly. If something were to malfunction, an aircraft log entry would be made to document the problem; a mechanic would replace the malfunctioning part, and the maintenance and engineering department will record the "write-up" in the central computer and compare the data with information gathered from other planes. Patterns and trends can become apparent *before* they become a problem. Engine performance is also documented on each and every flight approximately once an hour. The incredible reliability of modern turbofan engines can be attributed to three things: (1) the manufacturers are building state-of-the-art engines, (2) the powerplant mechanics who maintain the engines do a perfect job; and (3) regular engine-performance data is gathered and analyzed on a daily basis.

After a flight crew records the exact performance of all the engines, the people behind the scenes can computer analyze the data and determine if an engine is not running perfectly even though it is producing full power. An increase in oil or fuel consumption, slightly higher oil or exhaust gas temperatures, slightly lower power output at the same throttle position, etc. can all be signals. Long before the flight crew has an engine problem that would affect the flight, this slightly out of tune engine can be removed from the aircraft, replaced with a spare, and taken to the maintenance base for inspection and overhaul.

The newer aircraft that have the EICAS (Engine Indicating and Crew Alert System) computers are capable of automatically recording engine data, and faxing that information to a central maintenance base independent of any flight crew action while the airplane is still in-flight. It promises to further increase engine reliability.

PREVENTIVE MAINTENANCE

Preventive maintenance occurs before each flight. The exterior walkaround inspection, the interior safety inspection, and the cockpit acceptance check, are all examples of a routine trip check. If something is found marginally out of tolerance, the mechanics will replace that part from the parts inventory. Furthermore, all the newer aircraft have "status" computers that automatically alert the pilots and mechanics to a malfunction. Accessing this computer can simplify the troubleshooting and repair of a faulty system.

Once a day a more comprehensive preventive maintenance layover check is performed. Taking between two and five hours, depending on the size of the aircraft, this layover check is a detailed functional check of the aircraft. Even though everything may be normal, all the systems are operationally checked. The engine cowling—exterior chassis of the engine—is opened so a close inspection can be made. Inspection panels can be removed so the hard-to-see hidden components can be examined.

Service checks are performed every 100 hours of flight, on average every 10 days. This is similar to a layover check, but one step more thorough. Trip checks, layover checks, and service checks are performed each flight, daily, and every 100 hours respectively, for all make and models of aircraft.

Periodic checks—commonly referred to as letter checks because the required inspections are catalogued as A, B, C, etc.—are different. Specifically tailored to each different type of aircraft, this preventive maintenance program is designed by the manufacturers, airlines, and FAA jointly. This letter-check schedule requires progressive maintenance. The number of components and systems of the aircraft that must be inspected, repaired, or replaced each subsequent check increases with each trip to the hangar. For example, some aircraft require an A letter check after 300 hours of flight time. One item that must be checked is the landing gear. The B check might be required at 600 hours; requiring the inspection of the landing gear again, but also the landing gear doors and mechanisms. The C letter check will continue to increase the list. At approximately 18,000 hours of flight time, or 48 months, this preventive maintenance letter-check program culminates in a required complete overhaul of the aircraft.

OVERHAUL

An aircraft completing its required 18,000-hour overhaul is essentially a new airplane. During the four to six weeks—working twenty-four hours a day, seven days a week—that it takes to overhaul a commercial airliner, the plane is almost completely gutted and rebuilt. The airplane is disassembled, including removing the engines and landing gear. All the flight controls, cockpit instrumentation, and the passenger cabin are stripped to the bare metal fuselage. After everything (including the paint) is removed, the components are sent to the various specialty maintenance shops—hydraulic, electric, landing gear, metal, etc.— where all the parts are further disassembled, cleaned, inspected, repaired, reassembled, tested to the same tolerances and limits of a new item, and returned to the parts inventory if they pass, or are discarded. The remaining structure—basically the empty fuselage, wings, and tail—are themselves thoroughly tested. Something as minute as one faulty rivet will be replaced. Upon completion of all the checks and testing, the airplane is reassembled almost from the ground up. Except for the date on the original airworthiness certificate, it is sometimes difficult to tell a new aircraft from one just out of overhaul.

Any time an airplane is overhauled, it will be flown on a test flight with only pilots and mechanics on board. This two to four hour flight involves shutting down and restarting the engines in-flight; shutting down the hydraulics, turning off the electrics; basically checking all the systems and their primary, secondary, and backup features discussed throughout this book. After verifying that everything is 100 percent, the aircraft is certified fit to return to passenger service.

TYPES OF INSPECTIONS

Visiting an airline maintenance facility is more like visiting a hospital than the common misconception of a greasy machine shop. Some of the modern equipment used to maintain aircraft are very similar to the diagnostic equipment used by medical technicians and doctors. After visually checking the nuts and bolts and the other metal structural components, X-ray equipment is used to check the internal integrity and verify no hidden cracks are present. A small amount of electricity, called eddy currents, can be applied to the aluminum skin of the fuselage to ascertain that the structure is flawless. A tiny imperfection hidden beneath a rivet head, for example, will disrupt the even flow of electricity and register on the test equipment. Gyroscope equipment allows a magnified look at the inside of an engine without requiring any disassembly. Radio isotopes and dye penetrants can be injected into the engines and other systems to X-ray the nonmetal structures to obtain an even clearer picture of their "internal health."

Ultrasonic and acoustic emissions tests can be used to listen to the almost imperceptable "moans and groans" of the plane as it is physically twisted and stressed. Flaws as small as 50 one-thousandths of an inch can be detected long before they become any sort of hazard.

AIRWORTHINESS DIRECTIVES (A.D.'s)

As a further double-check that the commercial airline fleet is meticulously maintained, the FAA has set up an information system where maintenance reliability data can be shared by the airlines. If certain important components of an aircraft such as the engines, flight controls, hydraulic system, brakes, etc. should fail during flight, the individual airline must notify the FAA, which forwards the data to all airlines. This serves as an alert to the airlines so their inspection schedule can be altered as necessary. If another failure should occur with that same component, the FAA can order a mandatory change in the inspection timetable by issuing an Airworthiness Directive. Regardless of how soon the next preventive maintenance or overhaul is scheduled, an A.D. requires immediate action in the time allowed by the FAA, even if it requires removing an airplane from service. If an unsafe condition exists, an A.D. will be issued that will ground an entire fleet of airplanes, until a safe fix can be found.

All these maintenance inspections, and checks and balances within the system, are impressive. Regardless of cost, safety is and will always be the number-one goal of every responsible airline.

PART
II
The Flight

CHAPTER 9

PUSHBACK, ENGINE START, AND TAXI

Prior to the door being closed, the gate agent comes down the jetway and hands the captain the final paperwork. This includes the final passenger count—based on the tickets taken at the door—another current weather briefing forwarded by dispatch, and the final weight and balance data, which covers the number of passengers, the amount of fuel, the fuel distribution, the quantity of baggage and cargo, and whether there are any live animals in the cargo compartment.

In turn, the gate agent receives from the captain a signed flight dispatch release verifying he has received all the FAA-required documents and that his physical and mental health will allow him to successfully complete the flight.

CLOSING THE DOORS

Each door on the plane, including the cargo doors, contains a tiny micro switch which sends a signal to the cockpit indicating whether the door is open or closed and locked. If for some reason they are not closed and locked, the captain will ask the flight attendants to verify their position. If the cabin crew says the doors are closed and locked, but the cockpit indicator reads otherwise, a mechanic must be called.

ACTIVATING THE HYDRAULICS

Immediately prior to pushback the crew will turn on the hydraulic pumps and pressurize the hydraulic system to 3000 pounds per square inch (psi). This ensures the brakes are pressurized for pushback. As mentioned earlier, there are at least three hydraulic systems on every aircraft, and each system has multiple pumps located near the wheel well area. When operating, they create a noise that passengers often hear, an on and off whirl, as they cycle to maintain 3000 psi. This noise is continuous, however other noises act to mute the sound in flight.

SIGNALING THE GROUND CREW

In the moments before pushback the rotating beacons are turned on. Located on the top and bottom of the fuselage, these flashing red lights serve as anticollision beacons in flight. On the ground they are a signal to the ground crew personnel to stand clear, the aircraft is set to push or power back.

BLOCK TO BLOCK TIME

The average flight time from point A to point B can accurately be predicted by using the seasonally adjusted average headwinds or tailwinds and the cruising speed of the plane scheduled for the route. Flight time, however, does not completely reflect the total time, called the block to block time.

Though it may only take ten minutes to pushback and taxi to the active runway, the experienced traveler knows that during the busy travel hours, a line for departure is most probable. On the arrival end, it may only be a short taxi from the active runway to your gate, but ramp congestion may block immediate access. The airlines know all this and make allowances.

Average taxi times are computed—some up to 30 minutes at busy airports during busy times—and added to the flight time, which gives block to block time. This is what's reflected in timetables. Looking at a timetable, you may notice a midnight departure from New York to Chicago takes less time than the dinner flight. The difference is the built-in ground delay time. Sitting on a taxiway waiting for your turn for departure doesn't necessarily mean a late arrival.

COCKPIT ANNOUNCEMENTS

Before we talk about specific delays, let's mention why delay announcements from the cockpit sometimes seem late in coming. Early in a pilot's career, you learn to always tell the passengers the truth. But until specific information is known, pilots tend not to commit to an announcement that is less than accurate. Air Traffic Control, which has the ultimate say on departure, regardless of your schedule, is sometimes noncommittal when the weather is causing numerous flight delays.

CONNECTING FLIGHTS

Most airlines use a hub-and-spoke route structure, allowing more cities to receive more frequent service to more destinations. The downside is that more and more flights require a plane change to a connecting flight. With connections come some possible misconnections. Dispatch and the supervisors in charge of the release or holding of a flight for connecting passengers are connected via computer to the reservations system and are well aware of who is running late. In fact, a specific list of any late connecting passengers is sent to all the applicable departure gates. Factored into a difficult judgment call is how long the flight must be held, for how many people, and if this is the last flight of the day to your destination. It also must be determined if a wait for a few late connections will jeopardize all the downline connections of the passengers already on board.

OVERBOOKING AND NO-SHOWS

Overbooking is another reason for delays. On any given day, 10 percent of the people holding reservations don't show up. Around peak travel periods it is more. If a plane is only booked to capacity, every flight will depart with empty seats, even the busiest. If a flight is overbooked and the computer projection of no-shows is wrong, volunteers will be asked to get off in return for some form of compensation.

No-shows also affect the weight and balance planning for the flight. All airlines carry cargo in the same compartments used for luggage. If a plane is booked full space, weight limitations may dictate leaving some of the cargo for the next flight. However, if 45 passengers—15 percent of the capacity of a L-1011 or DC-10—do not show up, almost 9000 pounds of additional cargo can be carried. Again, last-minute work.

FINAL PAPERWORK

One of the most frustrating delays is waiting for all the required FAA paperwork from the gate agent, who wants no more than to release the plane on time. The same ground-based computers that are absolutely invaluable in running an airline play havoc with the system when they "go down." Most of the time the computer outages are only a matter of seconds until the backups come on line.

FUELING DELAYS

Fueling delays are sometimes encountered. Suppose the last-minute forecast for your destination is worse than originally anticipated. As discussed in the dispatch chapter, airlines always carry lots of "unanticipated delay" fuel plus some. If an in-flight delay becomes anticipated before departure, it is prudent to add fuel to cover that delay so as to not reduce your unanticipated quantity.

PASSENGERS SEATED

One of the simpler reasons for a delay in pushback is that not every passenger is seated with all their carry-on luggage properly stowed. The captain is subject to a $10,000 fine by the FAA if the aircraft is moved on the ground with people standing. This explains some of those rather direct announcements.

RAMP TOWER

Airlines, especially at the larger airports, exercise control over their own ramp areas or share the responsibility with the adjacent airline. At smaller airports the sequencing of aircraft is done by the ATC ground-control personnel in the control tower. If multiple airplanes wish to push back onto the same ramp area—or taxiway—at the same time, somebody has to wait. Sequencing of airplanes is beyond the pilot's control.

ANTI-ICE TRUCKS

As mentioned in Chapter 4, in cold, wintry weather, Type 1 de-icing fluid is good for 15 minutes prior to departure, and Type 2 is good for double that. Obviously, with a limited amount of time, the goal is to de-ice the planes as close to departure time as possible.

However, at some airports, where there are numerous flights scheduled within a short period of time, there may only be a handful of anti-ice trucks to service everyone. Having more is too costly, particularly in regions of the country with only occasional wintry weather. The car wash–like procedure now being used should reduce this problem.

FLOW CONTROL RESTRICTIONS

If Air Traffic Control anticipates any delays, mainly due to weather, that begin to approach 30 minutes, they will hold the aircraft at the gate ("gate-holds") to avoid the extra congestion in the air. It used to be that ATC exercised less scheduling control and allowed more aircraft to hold in the air. The new system of taking the delay on the ground rather than in the air does not affect your arrival time slot at your destination.

Flow control delays caused by the departure airport weather require the spacing between the departing aircraft to be increased. This decreases the number of departures per hour. Flow control restrictions caused by en route weather can be isolated over a particular area and may require only a change in flight plan route. Flow control restrictions caused by destination weather can be of the most concern for someone catching a connecting flight at that airport. However, any weather that affects your flight will most probably have affected the inbound leg of your connecting flight also.

PUSHBACK VERSUS POWERBACK

Some airlines push back their airplanes, some power back. The primary disadvantage of a pushback is the cost of investing in a tug, those powerful-looking, compact vehicles that tow airplanes in and out of the gates. These vehicles, weighing between 60,000 and 80,000 pounds, can generate 480 horsepower in first gear, giving them lots of torque or pushing power.

The major advantage to using these tugs is that the driver is an FAA-licensed mechanic who maintains contact with the flight crew, through headphones, until the engines are started and the engine generators and hydraulics are brought on line. If there are any last-minute problems, he can immediately begin discussing solutions.

However, because of the high cost of these tugs—upward of $75,000—many airlines have made it policy to power back their airplanes, which means actually putting the aircraft in reverse and backing away from the gate.

The disadvantage to this is having to start all the engines at the gate. High power is necessary, which requires extra caution in the gate area. Most aircraft are capable of sucking debris off the tarmac up to 16 feet in front of the engine. Debris sucked into an aircraft engine can cause damage.

ENGINE START

First you must have clearance. As just mentioned, turbo-fan engines have a danger zone of up to 16 feet in front, as well as hundreds of feet behind a running engine. Caution must be exercised.

All engines must be rotated or turned in order to start. A lawn mower uses a pull rope to start its engine. A car's battery provides the energy for the initial rotation. On an aircraft with jet engines, air is used.

On the ground, the APU is the primary source of compressed air, though an external air cart can be used as a substitute. By opening the start valves, APU air turns the starter, which begins the engine spinning. As the engine blades accelerate, they begin to draw the necessary ambient air into the combustion section of the engine for the start.

At approximately 25 percent of maximum engine RPM there is enough air in the multiple burner cans for a start. One of the two ignition systems is energized—to provide the heat—and the fuel valves are opened to complete the start.

As the engine accelerates to its ground idle RPM's of 40 to 60 percent, the starter is disengaged and the ignition is turned off. A jet engine is similar to your gas stove. You need the pilot light to initially ignite the gas flame on the burner, but once the flame is lit, the pilot light serves no purpose, except if a relight is necessary.

After the fuel and air are mixed and burned, their exhaust is routed across a two-stage exhaust turbine, causing it to turn. The exhaust turbine is mechanically connected back to the compressors in the front of the engine, causing them to turn, drawing more air into the engine for combustion, and the cycle continues. One reason aircraft engines are extremely reliable is that they have very few moving parts relative to the power they generate, and they only turn in one direction even during the use of reserve thrust on landing.

From your seat in the cabin a few things can be noticed during engine start. First, the APU only provides enough air for air-conditioning or engine start, and then just one engine at a time. All except the individual gasper fan above each seat must be turned off during the complete engine start cycle. First you will hear the air-conditioning being turned off, then, particularly during the summer, the cabin will become stuffier and warmer. Finally, the air-conditioning comes back on with more noise and more cooling flow than before the engine start.

Turbofan engines also have a unique rumble and whine as they start. With the starter turning the engine, the sound is hardly noticeable. However, when the fuel valves are opened and the engine accelerates toward idle RPM, a pitched rumble is quite distinct. Then, as the rotating parts of the engine stabilize, the rumble gives way to the familiar engine whine. On takeoff this same roar can be heard as the engines accelerate from idle to full takeoff power.

AFTER START CHECKLIST

In the cockpit there are multiple columns of engine gauges. One column for each engine. Each engine has two RPM gauges that indicate the rotation speed of the engine at two different locations. RPM's are given as percent of maximum, making it easier to read than your car's tachometer. An exhaust gas temperature gauge reads the temperature as it exits the "hot" section of the engine. Temperature limits power as well as RPM. Fuel flow meters measure the fuel consumption rate. Fuel flows can reach 18,000 pounds (2700 gallons per hour) per engine on fully loaded jumbo jets. Fortunately, those high power settings are only needed for takeoff and initial climb. Oil quantity, oil pressure, and oil temperature are familiar gauges. An engine pressure ratio (EPR) gauge is unique to aircraft. EPR is the ratio of the pressure exiting the engine compared to the initial pressure. Like a balloon that's not tied and let loose, the greater the pressure exiting, the more potential velocity. Engine vibration meters sense the smoothness of the engine at multiple locations. Like a tire, an engine out of balance needs repair. If there is a problem indicated by non-normal engine readings, the mechanic is available to inspect the engine to determine if it is a faulty gauge or something more substantial.

TAXI CLEARANCE

At large airports, ramp control clearance must be obtained to begin taxiing. When leaving the ramp area, ATC ground control has jurisdiction.

At smaller airports the ground controller located in the airport tower has the sole responsibility for airplane taxi flow. Larger airports have a ground radar system so they can "see" airplanes even in the fog.

ASSIGNING A RUNWAY

At airports with multiple runways, Air Traffic Control uses the general direction of your destination to decide which runway to assign you for take off.

At Miami, for example, there are two parallel runways aligned east and west, one north of the terminal and one south. Planes traveling to South America will be assigned the south runway. For aircraft destined for Chicago or Boston, ATC will assign the north complex. This sequencing on the ground helps the separation in the air by limiting cross traffic.

However, the south runway in Miami is longer than the north one. Since heavier planes need longer runways, northbound flights may request the south departure runway even if it means a delay. Some runways are smoother than others, causing less wear and tear, particularly on the tires, and it might be requested. Pilots can request the longest runway for any operational need, and at no time has ATC ever turned down the request.

TAXI OUT—FINDING YOUR WAY

All commercial airports have airport charts, which are essentially road maps illustrating the various runways and taxiways. The taxiways are labeled with letter identifiers, like Alpha, Bravo, Charlie, Delta, and Echo. After leaving the ramp area, the pilot calls ground control and says, "ABC flight number twelve," and ground control says, "Taxi to runway so and so," via "Taxiway Alpha to taxiway Bravo." If the airport is unfamiliar, pilots can then look on their maps to find their way.

During daytime the thick yellow taxiway center line is visible. At night the taxiways are illuminated with blue lights on the edge and green lights down the center. To prevent taxiing onto an active runway, one for which you've not been cleared, there are hold lines painted on the pavement. These cannot be crossed without obtaining clearance. Since these are difficult to see at night, these junctures also feature five amber lights running perpendicular to the taxiways. They indicate there is an active runway in front and permission is needed before taxiing onto or crossing it.

ACTUAL TAXI OUT

The taxi to the runway can occasionally feel a touch bumpy. Aircraft average 45,000 to 50,000 pounds of weight per each landing-gear tire, and though the concrete is almost two feet thick, this heavy tire footprint makes constant airport repairs necessary.

During taxi there seems to be constant acceleration and deceleration. But there's a reason for this. Aircraft engines have fairly high idles. A lightly loaded plane in particular requires very little additional power to start it rolling. And, unlike a car, when you take your foot off the gas —hand throttles, in the case of a plane—the aircraft may not slow right away. If you were to ride the brakes, they could become hot and less effective in case of an emergency stop.

The proper technique for taxiing a plane is to apply the brakes until the aircraft is traveling very slowly, release the brakes, let the plane reaccelerate, and repeat the procedure.

This maneuver is the most effective technique to keep your brakes their coolest.

The taxiways themselves are small compared to the size of a jumbo jet. Looking from a window seat, you can see the wings hang over the edge of a normal 75-foot-wide taxiway. And because the wheel track of the larger planes, like the 747, is up to 36 feet wide, a great deal of attention is required to keep the aircraft directly on the center line. Since the wheelbase—the distance from the nose wheel to the main landing gear—is up to 84 feet, particular skill is required to keep the plane on the center line throughout a sharp turn, which is one reason all passengers have to stay seated for taxi.

WHY FLIGHT ATTENDANTS TAKE THEIR SEATS DURING TAXI

After flight attendants have completed their safety-related duties, FAA regulations stipulate they remain in their seats throughout the duration of the taxi. Their primary responsibility after arming their emergency exit, and cross-checking across the aisle for the same, is to ensure that at least one flight attendant is available near every exit.

COCKPIT TAXI CHECKS

The captain taxis the airplane, using the taxi steering wheel located to his left, and separate from the flight controls. This steering mechanism, which on most aircraft is shaped like a tiller rather than a wheel, can hydraulically turn the nose wheel up to approximately 75 degrees left or right. Both the captain and co-pilot can taxi the plane straight, using the lower half of the rudder foot pedals. These pedals can turn the nose wheel up to 6 degrees left or right, sufficient for the takeoff and landing roll to be accomplished by either pilot. (As an option, a taxi tiller can be fitted on the co-pilot's side also.) The upper half of the same foot pedals controls the main gear brakes. Unlike a car, the left or right brakes can be applied independently to aid in making a tight turn.

While the captain is taxiing, the co-pilot is responsible for ramp tower, ground control, and tower communications, as well as completing—with the flight engineer on a three-person crew—the taxi procedures. When the captain is free of taxi distractions, the applicable written checklists are jointly used to verify that all the taxi checks have been accomplished.

All departure performance figures computed by central load control and dispatch are reviewed. Interestingly, all the computations are based on the unpleasant assumption that one engine will fail at the most inopportune time, just at liftoff. Every piece of data used by the flight crew, whether or not the runway is long enough for takeoff, whether or not the airplane can clear any and all obstacles at the end of the runway or in the airport vicinity, whether the plane can stop on the remaining runway during a takeoff abort, is all based on engine failure figures.

As we taxi out, the cockpit crew is double-checking the runway length, the aircraft's weight, and any local weather that could affect the takeoff.

Different weight limits are compared, and the most restrictive always apply. No matter how long the runway, each and every plane has a maximum weight it can safely lift and still meet all the emergency parameters. This maximum certified structural takeoff weight as defined by the manufacturers will never be exceeded. Most flights take off well below the maximum gross weight.

Airplanes closer to their maximum weight will require more runway than when the plane is lighter. It is inaccurate to assume a big plane like a 767 takes more runway than a smaller DC-9. A 767 is indeed bigger and heavier, but the engines are correspondingly more powerful; therefore, the thrust-to-weight ratio remains similar.

Takeoff limits are subdivided into runway and climb

limits. Runway limits define the maximum this particular plane can weigh and still be accelerated to takeoff speed, an emergency abort made, and the plane safely stopped.

Climb limits define the maximum this plane can weigh, be accelerated to takeoff speed, have a catastrophic engine failure, and still climb and clear all obstacles.

Hot humid days and departures from high-elevation airports require longer takeoff runs. Headwinds are advantageous, increasing the runway allowable weights approximately 700 pounds for every knot of headwind. Tailwinds require penalties, up to 3500 pounds for every knot up to the maximum legal tailwind limit of 10 knots. Crosswinds are allowed, but the 90-degree crosswind component cannot exceed the crosswind limit of the airplane, which by FAA certification standards must be no less than 25 knots. Runways that are wet can be slippery; a 15 percent margin of safety must be added.

FLAP SETTINGS

Once the various limits are double-checked, the proper flap setting must be determined. Most airliners have a choice between two settings, 5 and 15 degrees.

"Flaps 15," the normal takeoff position on most aircraft, provides a great deal of additional lift. This flap setting provides the quickest and shortest ground run.

"Flaps 5," requires a longer takeoff roll, because the lesser flap setting means a greater takeoff speed is required; however, the additional speed offers a greater initial climb gradient.

Full power or a lesser alternate power takeoff may be made. If weather, runway length, climb gradient, or any MEL (Minimum Equipment List) restrictions were a factor, full power would always be used. Alternate power is only considered when the aircraft's actual weight is well below any legal limits. Adhering to very strict guidelines, an alternate power setting can be used primarily for noise abatement and reducing engine wear.

Any alternate power setting must still meet all the safety criteria governing engine failure at the most critical time, and be able to do so without increasing the power, though that option remains.

TAKEOFF SPEEDS

Takeoff speeds are directly proportional to the aircraft's weight, adjusted for factors such as power setting, flap setting, runway condition, temperature, and departure airport elevation. The three critical speeds are V-1, V-R, and V-2.

The V-1 (velocity-1) speed, calculated from tables on board the plane, is the maximum accelerate-stop speed. A decision to abort a takeoff must be made before the V-1 speed. An abort above the V-1 speed does not guarantee enough time to decelerate to a complete stop on the remaining runway, therefore the aircraft is committed to takeoff. V-R is the initial rotation speed, the speed at which the airplane begins its actual takeoff. Quick calculations will show you that on exceptionally long runways, V-1 can sometimes be a higher speed than the V-R speed. Since an aborted takeoff would never be attempted after the nose has been raised off the ground, V-1 and V-R in this case would be the same.

The V-2 speed is the single-engine climb speed. If a critical engine should fail at or above the V-1 speed, the V-2 speed will provide the best rate of climb.

FLIGHT CONTROL CHECKS

During taxi it is vital to check each and every flight control, making certain they are operating through their complete range. Since the crew has very limited, if any, view of the wings, and no view of the tail, flight control position gauges are installed. When passengers see the spoiler panels and ailerons move up and down during taxi, what they are seeing is the pilot checking the controls.

CABIN VISITS

If the pilots—mindful of the 15- to 30-minute time span crucial during de-icing—suspect any ice buildup, one flight crew member goes to the cabin windows as nonchalantly as possible, and verifies that the wings are completely free of frost and wet snow. If they are not, further de-icing is necessary. The term *wet snow* is important here. On very cold days dry snow can accumulate on the wings, but the frigid cold prevents any of it from sticking, and it will easily blow off on the initial takeoff run. Any doubts about wet or dry and it's back to the de-ice trucks.

TAKEOFF SIGNALS

There are two ways the pilots can notify the flight attendants that it is close to departure time. One, if time permits, is a public address announcement ending with something like, "Will the flight attendants please prepare the cabin for departure." If the cockpit crew is busy with a checklist, or talking with ATC, then communications between the cockpit and cabin is done with chimes. Two bells indicates that only a few minutes remain before departure. The flight attendants will double-check, but it is the passengers' responsibility to ensure that their seat belts are securely fastened, their seatbacks and tray tables in their full upright position, and all carry-on luggage properly stowed under the seat in front of them or in a closed overhead bin.

CONTROL TOWER

With the engines started, the flight attendants seated, and all the checklists complete, all that is left is to wait for our turn for departure. The radios are switched from the ground control frequency to the tower, which is responsible for controlling all takeoff and landing clearances. On a runway used primarily for takeoffs, departures can average nearly one a minute. On a runway used for both arrivals and departures, no one will quarrel with the fact that inbound flights have priority.

CHAPTER 10

TAKEOFF AND DEPARTURE

Takeoff is the most critical phase of flight because the greatest stress is imposed on the plane. The engines are running at full power. The airframe, including the landing gear and tires, are carrying their largest load. Also, any abnormality must be handled at low altitude. This is why a significant portion of recurrent training—the mandatory simulator checks required of pilots every six months—is spent learning to respond to takeoff emergencies.

WHO FLIES THE PLANE?

Under normal circumstances, the captain flies one leg of a trip and the co-pilot flies the next. Why do they rotate actual flying responsibilities back and forth? If the captain were to make every takeoff and landing, then the co-pilot would have no experience. Still, the captain, who has ultimate responsibility for the passengers and the plane, has final authority over whether he or the first officer flies the plane. Certain weather conditions, such as low visibility, require that the captain take the controls.

119

LEGAL FOR TAKEOFF

Before a plane can take off, three criteria must be satisfied: the pilots must be legal, the plane must be legal, and the airport itself must be legal.

Of course, the pilots must have current FAA licenses, including their FAA physical certificate and FCC radiotelephone license. They must also be up-to-date on their simulator proficiency and airplane line checks. Without these, they need not show up for work.

But what it means for a pilot to be legal has to do with visibility requirements. No matter the co-pilot's experience, when the visibility is less than 1600 feet, or a quarter mile, the captain must make the takeoff.

The plane itself must also be legal. This means all the systems and their backups are functioning normally.

The greatest variable in this equation is the airport being legal. Even different runways at the same airport can have different restrictions. Runway takeoff minimums, for example, contain numerous variables.

RUNWAYS (AND WEATHER)

Runways earn the lowest visibility requirement, currently 600 feet runway visual range (RVR), by having a complete set of painted runway markings clearly depicting such things as the runway's center line. Runway lighting, which depicts the same things but is easier to see in reduced visibility, must also be available. Runway center-line and edge lighting is color coded: the last 3000 feet are amber, the last 2000 feet are red and white, and the final 1000 feet are all red so that it's distinct.

An RVR system that reads the specific visibility must also be operating. This system reads three zones: the touchdown, which is the first one-third; the midfield, which is the middle third; and the roll out, which is the last third. The system must show that all three zones are above the 600-foot minimum.

If any part of the runway is not operating correctly, from the center-line lights to one of the RVR meters, the takeoff minimum is raised. On a runway with paint-only markings, the takeoff minimum is one-quarter mile.

Although snow, rain, and ice may not reduce visibility below the legal limits, they do create restrictions. All runways are crowned, meaning higher in the center, and grooved, meaning troughs are cut across the width every few inches, to allow rapid water runoff. Still, standing water can accumulate, so a legal limit of one-half inch maximum is mandated.

Wet, slushy snow also imposes limits, since it retards acceleration on takeoff. Again there is a one-half inch maximum. Dry, powdery snow is different. As long as there is enough friction between the ground and the wheels to allow for normal acceleration and braking, a maximum of six inches of dry snow is allowed on the runway. Ice on the runway is never permitted.

PRE-TAKEOFF BRIEFING

Before taking the active runway, the cockpit crew discusses all the routine procedures as well as all the what-ifs they might encounter. Although pilots all go through the same training, if a quick decision has to be made, this pre-departure briefing helps to maximize the crew's response.

TALKING WITH THE CONTROL TOWER

As the plane approaches the runway, ground control reconfirms its takeoff slot and instructs the pilot to contact the tower. The tower Air Traffic Controllers are directly responsible for all takeoff and landing clearances, any taxi clearances on or across an active runway, and traffic separation within the airport's traffic area, a radius of approximately five miles.

When a plane is number one in line for takeoff, one of three tower instructions will be transmitted:

1. If a plane is landing on that runway, the tower will say "Hold Short."
2. If a plane has just landed but has yet to exit the runway, or a prior airplane is taking off but not yet airborne, the clearance will be "Taxi into position and hold." This allows the plane to taxi onto an active runway but not depart.
3. The tower will say "Cleared for takeoff."

But several criteria must be met before a plane is cleared for takeoff. First, the runway must be completely cleared—which means no planes exiting or taxiing. Second, the preceding departure must be far enough in front that there is no possible chance of catching up to it. Departures behind so-called "heavy" planes, those having a gross weight in excess of 300,000 pounds, require added caution. All aircraft produce mini artificial tornadoes called wake turbulence—or wing-tip vortices—just like a speedboat leaves a disturbance in the water. Departing behind a "heavy" requires spacing of no less than two minutes or five miles.

CLEARED FOR TAKEOFF

Pilots can employ two different types of takeoff—either a static or a rolling takeoff.

In a static takeoff, meaning from a stopped position, it is most common for the brakes to be released, power slowly applied, and the takeoff roll begun. It's preferred when visibility is reduced or when a runway is not completely bare and dry. Also, if the plane is cleared to taxi into position and then hold, a static takeoff is the only choice.

Rolling takeoffs are ordinarily made when the tower clears the plane for takeoff from the Hold Short line. Less power is needed to start the takeoff roll, which reduces the jet blast behind the engines. For this reason, at some airports where the runways are very near highways, rolling takeoffs are mandatory. Rolling takeoffs are also made because the less time each individual plane spends on the runway, the greater the airport's capacity. But a pilot can request either a static or rolling takeoff, as necessary.

LIGHTS

While waiting for departure, the crew will turn off the plane's lights, which are especially noticeable at night from window seats. Since most taxiways face directly toward the approach areas, any arriving planes would find the bright lights a nuisance. When cleared for takeoff, the full complement of lights, including the wing-tip strobe lights, are turned on.

HOW DOES AIR TRAFFIC CONTROL SEE THE PLANE?

In good weather conditions ATC can see a plane when it's on the ground or near the airport simply by looking out the window. But to supplement this rather limited technique, every commercial airliner has a transponder and encoding altimeter. The pilot enters a distinct four-digit code into this cockpit instrument, which sends the aircraft's exact location and altitude—to within 100 feet—to all ground stations within radio range. When the tower controller matches the specific flight with its distinct code, the two are tagged together the entire flight. Any ATC facility with radar, towers, approach and departure control at airports and the various en route centers can see the plane even if it's not in direct voice communication. All aircraft—large or small, commercial or private—must have transponders when operating near airports with TCA's (Terminal Control Areas) and when cruising above 12,500 feet.

In the event the transponder should malfunction, an independent backup can be turned on.

TAKEOFF

Power is controlled by the multiple thrust levers—depending on the number of engines—located on the throttle quadrant between the pilots. Pushing the thrust levers forward increases power, pulling them all the way back to the stop decreases power to idle. Big turbofan engines take a few seconds to accelerate from idle, so to ensure that all the engines are developing power at the same rate, the thrust levers are first moved only partway forward. Asymmetric thrust would make initial directional control more difficult. Like a turbo charger in a car, a turbofan engine is slower accelerating from idle to 50 percent power, than from 50 percent to full power. Therefore, care must be taken not to overspeed—over-rev in your car—your engine. Newer planes have Electronic Engine Controls (EEC's) that can automatically prevent overspeed, but do not yet have the capability of preventing excessive temperatures. Similar to initial taxiing, the sounds generated from the engine will begin with a deep rumble as the fan, compressors, and turbines spin up at slightly different rates, followed by the familiar whine of a stabilized and smoothly running machine. Full power must be set before accelerating through 60 knots.

Immediately after applying full power, the engine instruments are thoroughly checked. The pilot not flying will verify that all the engine gauges are within specific parameters. A unique feature of the engine instruments is that all the gauges are designed so at full power all the needles point to the nine o'clock position. After the engines have stabilized during initial power application, the autothrottles are capable of setting the power with computerized precision. However, as a safety against a computer glitch causing the power to be reduced at an inopportune time, when accelerating through 80 knots the autothrottles drop into a "throttle hold," or manual mode. This allows an increase or decrease in power to be made independent of the computer.

Accelerating to liftoff speed, passengers—particularly near the front of the plane—hear and feel a thump-thump-thump. This is the tires going over the center-line lights. The center-line lights are raised slightly above the surface of the runway in order that they can be seen from great horizontal distances. If they were mounted flush, they would only be visible from directly overhead—not very useful for approach and landing. Tracking exactly on the center line, this slight bump every 75 feet can be felt. The lights are built to withstand a direct 300-ton load. Steering slightly left or right of center line will stop this inconsequential thumping.

Passengers sometimes express concern to the flight attendants that the overhead interior panels seem to vibrate on takeoff. These panels, constructed of lightweight composite materials, are installed for cosmetic reasons only. Like a drop ceiling in an office, they cover up the plumbing, air-conditioning ducts, and the various wiring that runs the course of the plane. Their removal allows easy access for any required maintenance. The shaking and vibration is normal.

Accelerating through 85 knots, the rejected takeoff automatic brakes that were previously armed become active. At this point if the thrust levers are retarded to idle, maximum braking will automatically be initiated. The one- or two-second reaction-time advantage the autobrakes have over manual braking by the pilots can mean a shorter stopping distance of several hundred feet. It also means that any aborted takeoff above 85 knots (98 mph) will be fairly dramatic, because unlike the pilots, the autobrakes cannot tell how much runway remains.

Approaching 100 knots (115 mph), a double-check of the engine instruments will be made, if it hasn't already been done. Acceleration time can be compared to the predicted standards; zero to 100 knots usually takes between 20 and 30 seconds, depending on the aircraft's weight.

Passing V-1—approximately 130 knots (150 mph)—the plane is committed to takeoff. At this point all the performance data guarantees acceleration to V-2 (140 knots, 161 mph), engine failure climb speed. At V-R (approximately 135 knots, 155 mph), the calculated velocity of rotation, the nose wheel is rotated skyward at 3 degrees per second. Slower rotations are acceptable, though they use additional runway. Faster rotations are avoided, because of the chance of a tail strike if the nose of the plane is rotated higher than 11 degrees before the main gear flies off the ground. In the unlikely event of a tail strike, the tail is fitted with a compressible tail skid that acts as a shock absorber.

Initial climb is accomplished at V-2 plus 10 knots (or 150 knots, 173 mph), to maximize the initial rate of climb.

GEAR UP

Once airborne, the thump-thump of the runway is replaced by the smooth sense of flight. The airplane is finally in the environment for which it was built.

Immediately after liftoff, passengers can sense the extension of the landing gear shock-absorbing struts. The landing gear is extremely heavy, and once the weight of the plane is removed, the struts are designed to fully extend. On bogie gear—landing gear with more than two tires—the entire mechanism tilts as well as extends. In this fully extended (and tilted) position, the gear fits into the wheel wells. The landing gear is a high-drag item and serves no purpose in flight. With a positive rate of climb indicated on the vertical speed instrument, and then called by the pilot not flying, the command for gear up is made. The gear handle is raised from down to the up position.

The first sound heard by the passengers is the gear doors opening. With the doors opened, the gear is hydraulically raised into its wheel wells. During retraction, the main gear brakes are automatically applied to stop the tire rotation. Once fully retracted, the gear doors close again. There is one unique difference about the nose gear: Since that gear has no brakes, the tire rotation is stopped with a rubber snubber mounted in the nose-wheel well. This snubbing sound can be quite loud, but lasts only a moment or two.

ABORTED TAKEOFFS

According to a study completed in 1987, takeoff is aborted in about one in every 300,000 flights. This, however, does not give a complete picture. Some aborts are at speeds well below a critical speed, and most aborts are for reasons other than an engine problem. Those of most concern are at or near the critical V-1 accelerate-stop speed. High-speed aborts are difficult. If a warning light comes on, you have to assume the worst and abort if your speed is below V-1.

There is little or no time to assess the situation. Consequently, aborts have been made for nuisance cautions and alerts. On newer aircraft this problem is being rectified. Unlike older planes, when the newer ships accelerate through 80 knots, the malfunction of a nonessential item will not be indicated by the usual caution lights, horns, or buzzers until 20 seconds or the first 400 feet of flight.

If, for example, a fuel pump were to fail at or near V-1, there's another fuel pump to do the job, making this a noncritical item during takeoff. Despite the failure, there is no need to abort takeoff. Instead of a high-speed abort, the safer procedure is to circle back and land. On these new high-technology aircraft, the computers have prioritized the warnings, reducing the need to analyze before acting.

ENGINE FAILURE DURING TAKEOFF

The most critical time for an engine failure is exactly at V-1, a moment before takeoff. Pilots know it, airline training departments train for it, airplane and engine manufacturers design for it, and performance data is figured with it. A worst-case scenario is always assumed.

If an engine failed, the plane would circle once around the traffic pattern and return for landing. If the airport were closed, an alternate landing airport would have already been decided. Again, the airplane is able to fly just fine with an engine shutdown. It was designed to do so. But again, as a precaution, the flight attendants will brief everyone about the applicable emergency procedures.

Suppose an engine caught fire? As a safety measure, aircraft engines (both wing and tail) are mounted on struts to isolate them from the main body of the plane. Fires can be extinguished, first, by closing multiple fuel valves with the pull of one fire handle and removing all the fuel going to the affected engine. Also, the engine can be starved of oxygen by discharging one or both fire extinguishers directly into the engine. This is done by rotating that same fire handle left or right. After the fire is out, the same engine failure procedures are followed.

Hard as it is to imagine, birds can cause an engine shutdown. Not one, two, or three birds, but an entire flock. Airports, with their vast empty spaces, serve as convenient stopover points for migrating birds. The loud noise of the jet engines usually frighten them away before takeoff. However, at some airports remote mini-cannons firing blanks are needed to clear the takeoff zone. Birds in flight can sense the plane approaching, and make every effort to fly clear, but some occasionally do hit the airplane and bounce clear. The critical problem is when birds are ingested into the engines. Several birds at once, or many birds over a short period of time, will be chopped up quite completely and exhausted out the back of the engine with no damage to the aircraft. However, a flock of birds going through the engine at once can overload the engine compressor, nicking one of the blades, causing an out-of-balance vibration. A precautionary engine shutdown and return to the departure airport may be necessary.

INITIAL CLIMB

For passenger comfort, the initial angle of climb is limited to 18 to 20 degrees nose up, even if the airspeed accelerates beyond V-2 plus 10 knots. This rapid rate of climb is continued to 1000 feet AGL (above ground level). At 1000 feet AGL, the nose of the aircraft is lowered to approximately 10 to 12 degrees nose up, so the plane can be accelerated. At this point the power is reduced from takeoff to a climb power setting and can be heard. The amount of power reduction is dependent on the specific noise abatement procedure.

With airspeed increasing through 160 to 170 knots (again depending on weight), flap retraction is started. The pilot flying calls for the appropriate flap setting, and the other pilot actually moves the flap level to provide an airspeed double-check. Flaps are raised from their takeoff position of 15 degrees to 5 degrees. Looking out the window, you can see the flaps retract, and you can hear the hydraulic motors operating in the wheel wells. As the airspeed increases further to the 180 to 190 knot range, the flaps are raised further, to a 1 or 2 degree position—essentially up—leaving only the leading edge slats deployed. Reaching the 210 to 220 knot range, the high lift devices—flaps and slats—are completely raised to the zero or up position. With the flaps and slats fully retracted, the airplane is said to be in the "clean configuration," and any induced vibration from the additional drag will cease.

Complete cleanup is accomplished during the first 3000 feet of climb—the first couple of minutes of flight. At 3000 feet above the ground, additional climb power may be added to increase the acceleration rate without violating the airport good neighbor policies.

Acceleration is completed to 250 knots (288 mph), the maximum allowable ATC speed until climbing through 10,000 feet. Just like accelerating onto an interstate, a rapid acceleration allows more room for the planes following, increasing airport capacity.

Sometimes on the initial climb to 3000 feet, the air is a bit choppy even though the wind is calm. Why? Just like swirling air currents created by tall buildings, convective air currents can be present. The large, open concrete expanse of an airport surrounded by industrial plants or other buildings can cause uneven heating of the earth's surface, and mild chop. Air currents caused by the friction between the earth and the atmosphere as the earth rotates can also cause low-level convective air. In any case, with initial rates of climb anywhere from 1500 to up to 4000 feet per minute (with a light load), this low-level chop, if still present, is very short-lived.

At 10,000 feet the speed limit is lifted, which means the nose will again be lowered to approximately 5 degrees nose up and the aircraft is allowed to accelerate to its best climb speed of around 300 to 320 knots. With the body angle of the plane reduced, and no choppy air forecast, the flight attendants will begin cabin service and the seat-belt light will be turned off.

CHAPTER 11

CLIMB, CRUISE, AND DESCENT

This chapter will concentrate on the body of the flight, the portion where the airplane climbs above 10,000 feet on departure, the en route cruise, and the descent to the terminal arrival area, 10,000 feet above and 20 to 40 miles from the destination airport.

STERILE COCKPIT RULE

When the plane is moving on the ground, and when it's below 10,000 feet, the cockpit crew is prohibited by FAA law from any extraneous communication not relating to the safety of the flight. This is known as the Sterile Cockpit Rule. It's intended to reduce pilot workload during the busiest portions of the flight. A literal interpretation makes announcements to the passengers—choppy air, unusual departure procedure, a plane nearby flying a parallel route, go-arounds on approach, and sightseeing narrations—all illegal when below 10,000 feet. There are many times a simple explanation would ease some concern. Pilots know this. But the Sterile Cockpit Rule prohibits it.

AIR TRAFFIC CONTROL (ATC) AND TRAFFIC SEPARATION

The only technique pilots have for avoiding a midair collision is to "see and avoid." When the planes are close to airports, flying at relatively slow speeds and with good visibility, visual separation is safe. At higher flight levels and greater speeds, "see and avoid" does not provide anywhere near the margin of safety required. Consequently, the responsibility for traffic separation rests with Air Traffic Control.

As stated earlier, every plane is equipped with electronic devices that send ATC an exact location and altitude, accurate to within 100 feet. After a distinct four-digit code is entered into the on-board transponder, the flight is positively tagged and followed by the ATC ground computers. As the coded blip passes across the Air Traffic Controller's radar scope, he can see both the plane's exact current position and its anticipated location in any selected time frame. The current speed, direction, and rate of altitude change are all displayed and updated every few seconds.

There are 20 separate Air Traffic Control centers throughout the 48 states. Each center is subdivided into multiple sectors with different radio frequencies. Though pilots talk with one portion of an ATC center at a time, their radar blip can be seen on multiple radar scopes simultaneously. In fact, long before radio frequency is changed from one controller to the next, radar contact will already have been established.

CONFLICT ALERT (TRAFFIC SEPARATION)

In good weather all aircraft within the terminal radar area are kept a minimum of three miles apart. In bad weather, the distance is greater. Leaving the airport vicinity, the minimum separation distance increases to five miles.

With increasing speeds and higher altitudes, the minimum separation can increase to 10 to 20 miles. It is not uncommon during thunderstorm season, when a great deal of circumnavigation is required to stay clear of any intense rainshowers, for the minimum distance to increase to 50 miles. The weather conditions and traffic congestion dictate the traffic separation necessary.

If the ATC computers ever sense that within the next two minutes airplanes will get closer than the prescribed minimum limits, their computers will indicate a conflict alert. Both an aural and visual radar-scope warning alert the Air Traffic Controller to increase the separation. They would immediately communicate with one or both aircraft and direct them to turn, climb, or descend.

Air Traffic Controllers face discipline for allowing unexplained conflict alerts. Therefore, if the required minimum separation is five miles, ATC will keep them a significantly greater distance apart, allowing for an even bigger margin of error.

Traffic Alert and Collision Avoidance System (TCAS) is an additional safety feature that will be installed on all commercial aircraft by the end of 1993. At present, only ground-based radar sites can receive and interpret transponder and encoding altimeter information. But the new TCAS will make it possible for all airliners to see the radar blip of all nearby planes long before they could be visually sighted. If a conflict is sensed by the airborne system, a warning will not only alert the pilots, but the two TCAS systems will interpret each other's telemetry information and issue specific avoidance instructions.

PITCH ATTITUDE—CLIMB SPEED

As the airplane climbs through 10,000 feet, the most noticeable change in the cabin will be the pitch attitude. Up to this attitude, ATC limits all aircraft to a 250 knot (288 mph) speed restriction, since there are more planes in less airspace at the lower altitudes. When the 250-knot speed restriction is lifted, the pilots will accelerate to a more efficient cruise climb speed of 300 to 320 knots. To accelerate, both the climb power will be increased and the angle of climb decreased. The power change can be heard and the decrease of pitch felt as it lowers from more than 10 degrees nose up to a more level-feeling 5 degrees.

POSITIVE CONTROL AREA

Federal Aviation Regulations define two distinct methods of flying: (1) by visual reference only—looking outside —or (2) by instrument reference, where no outside visibility is required.

Regardless of visibility, commercial airlines are required to always operate IFR (Instrument Flight Rules). If visibility is good, it makes for a more pleasant flight, but being able to see outside is not necessary. Flying under IFR rules, whether or not visibility is good, requires full ATC clearance and positive transponder identification.

Above 18,000 feet the airspace is known as the Positive Control Area. All flights, private and commercial, must operate under full IFR rules. Most of the little private aircraft are not capable of flying that high, but many charter, corporation, and commuter planes are. To ensure the full traffic avoidance, ATC must be utilized. Above 18,000 feet no exceptions to the full IFR rules are made.

CABIN PRESSURE

The pressurization system is capable of maintaining sea-level cabin pressure up to a flight altitude of about 24,000 feet. However, if your cruising altitude is 35,000 feet, and the cabin pressure is held at sea level until 24,000 feet, all the internal cabin pressure change would be concentrated in the last 11,000 feet of climb, which might be uncomfortable. Instead, the cabin altitude begins climbing very slowly immediately after takeoff.

Rates of internal cabin pressure change are kept to 500 feet per minute while going up and 300 feet per minute while coming down. This is less than the rate of change in many high-rise building elevators. At cruising flight levels the cabin altitude averages 6000 to 7000 feet.

Some passengers find it harder to clear their ears on descent rather than when the craft is climbing. Flight attendants are trained in various helpful techniques, such as squeezing your nostrils and blowing lightly, swallowing, chewing, and placing warm compresses on your ears. These techniques work best if started early in descent.

STEP CLIMB

Airplanes are capable of climbing from takeoff to their initial cruising altitude without ever leveling off. But on most flights ATC restrictions prevent this. Pilots prefer a rapid climb to at least 10,000 feet because it gets you above most light aircraft and does not require large climb-power adjustments.

However, there are times, because of conflicting traffic and/or delayed radar hand-offs from one ATC facility to another, when altitudes are held down. These "hold down" altitudes result in step climbs.

Just like a set of stairs, planes climb and level off, climb and level off. If ATC clears a plane to 5000 feet, it will climb to that altitude and accelerate to 250 knots. Once level "at five," a sizable power reduction will be made in order not to exceed the 250 knots-below-10,000-feet speed limit. Once cleared higher, the climb power will be restored to maximize the rate of climb. If another hold-down altitude is issued, the power will be significantly reduced again and reapplied when further climb clearance is received.

As mentioned, all Air Traffic Control centers are divided into sectors, though some sector divisions are geographic and others are dictated by altitude. Climbing through 23,000 feet requires a transition from the low altitude to high altitude Air Traffic Controller. Since the high altitude controller has to fit you in with all the aircraft already at cruise, a temporary altitude limit of 23,000 feet is usually issued until higher altitude airspace is available. This requires another step climb.

As the plane climbs to the flight levels in the 35,000 foot range, step climbs are self-imposed. Heavily loaded airplanes, with a full complement of fuel and cargo, may be altitude limited. When the weight of the plane is reduced by fuel usage, a step climb to a higher, more efficient altitude will be requested. Long overseas flights, with very heavy fuel loads, require multiple step climbs.

CRUISE ALTITUDE—PITCH OF THE PLANE

Approaching cruise altitude, the pitch of the airplane, which has been approximately 5 degrees nose up, will again be lowered to stop the climb. If cruising at maximum airspeed, the angle of pitch required to maintain level flight is small. Flying at speeds slightly slower than max cruise— for increased fuel economy—requires a slight nose-up pitch from 1 to 3 degrees. The pitch attitude is adjusted according to speed in order to maintain level flight.

Climbing through 18,000 feet, the plane enters the Positive Control Area, where all flights are conducted under IFR rules. Also above 18,000 feet, altitudes become Flight Levels (FL). For example, 25,000 feet becomes FL 250. The difference lies in how the barometric altimeter is set to measure altitude. Below 18,000 feet the altimeter must constantly be updated to reflect the local barometric pressure, so a true measure of altitude above sea level is read on the gauge. Above 18,000 feet in the United States, terrain avoidance is not a hazard, except in some locations over Alaska. Traffic separation is the priority, so instead of having all the airplanes continually resetting their barometric altimeters, everyone uses the standard pressure setting of 29.92 inches of mercury. What this means is that FL 250 is not exactly 25,000 feet if the pressure is anything but standard. The amount of variation is exactly the same for all aircraft.

As planes fly through areas of changing pressures, their flight level remains exactly the same, but their true altitude above sea level gradually changes. They will be gradually climbing and descending, which is hardly detectable, however the power changes necessary to hold a constant airspeed may be noticeable.

NAVIGATION

Most aerial navigation is done on a point-to-point basis. A 2000-mile flight may involve ten 200-mile segments. In the United States there are over 700 ground-based VOR (Very High Frequency Omnidirectional Range) stations, all spaced at intervals. Connecting all these VOR stations are airways, highways in the sky. These airways are clearly defined, just like a road, and labeled on aeronautical charts. If the airway is below 18,000 feet, it is called a Victor (V) airway; above 18,000 feet, a Jet (J) airway. Navigating across the United States is quite similar to reading a road map. You start off at your home, and have to make lots of turns on smaller roads to reach a boulevard. The boulevard leads to the interstate, and you can finally drive a fairly straight course. In an airplane we do much the same. We fly departure routes, to the low altitude Victor airways, and then the Jet routes.

VOR's send out radio signals in all directions. The more powerful VOR signals can be received up to 230 nautical miles, meaning two stations 460 miles apart can define an airway. The signal the VOR sends is unique for every degree of the compass. The aircraft's on-board VOR receiver can accurately pinpoint where you are in relation to the station. This position from the station is called a radial. By using two VOR's and determining exactly where the radials cross, you would know exactly where you are. Most stations also have a DME (Distance Measure Equipment) co-located at the VOR. By using one VOR to determine the radial from the station, and the DME to determine the distance, you can also pinpoint your position.

All airways are defined by specific radials. Flying from point A to point B, we fly outbound from one VOR on a specific radial (airway) to intercept the inbound radial to the next VOR. Cross the second VOR, and fly outbound on another predetermined radial, until a third VOR is within reception range. This continues until the aircraft reaches the arrival route to its destination.

During times of the day when ATC is not as busy, direct routing between more distant VOR's can be approved. By eliminating the small zigs and zags of the airway system— no different than the small turns on the interstate—a few miles can be saved.

The next step in saving en route time, other than flying faster, is to fly the shortest distance between the departure and destination airport. This shortest distance is called the great circle route. Since the earth is round, the shortest distance between two points is a line that would appear as an arc on a flat map. Departing New York and flying east-northeast the entire flight, will take you to Paris. However, departing New York farther northeast bound, making an almost undetectable gradual turn to the east, and then flying southeast to arrive in Paris, is shorter by 127 miles. As a rule of thumb for east or westbound flights, the longer the flight the closer to the poles you will fly, to minimize the distance.

When flying a great circle route, special navigational equipment is required since the aircraft's compass heading is constantly changing. An Inertial Reference System (IRS), and an Inertial Navigational System (INS) are the two most common long-range navigational systems in use today. Both these systems share the basic principal that if you enter into the computers exactly where you are while parked at the departure gate, where you want to fly, the great circle route will automatically be computed. Since these systems are completely independent of any ground-based radio signals, a minimum of three INS, or INS units, are required for cross-checking information and redundancy. The information computed by these systems can be displayed to the pilots on a conventional VOR left/right needle, or a cathode ray tube Flight Management System (FMS) found on the newer aircraft. In either case, to keep the airplane exactly on course, a constantly changing heading is necessary. On many flights, rhumb line (the one compass-course line) and great circle route courses are both utilized. Rhumb lines are used for the shorter segments and when ATC uses preplanned airways for traffic separation. Great circle routes are used on long hauls if the aircraft is so equipped.

AUTOPILOT

An autopilot is essentially a stabilizing system that's capable of flying the airplane when the correct inputs are made. It relieves the pilots from the constant fine-tuning of the flight controls.

However, the autopilot is shrouded in a bit of a myth. Despite its complex computer system, the autopilot has no brain. It is capable of flying the airplane in climb, cruise, descent, approach, and sometimes landing, but only if the pilot tells it what to do. You can tell an autopilot to fly a specific heading and/or a specific altitude, and it will monitor itself to maintain those parameters. That's it. On newer plans the autopilot does a magnificent job of flying nearly the entire flight-plan route—as long as it's programmed to exact specifications. If there is bad weather ahead, a change in route or altitude, airspeed changes for traffic separation, the pilot must tell the autopilot a change is needed.

One essential convenience provided by the autopilot is its ability to constantly trim the plane along its longitudinal (pitch) axis. During flight, the aircraft's center of gravity, its center of weight, is constantly changing in small increments as passengers move around, flight attendants wheel the galley carts up and down the aisles, and fuel is used. Pitch changes are constantly needed to maintain a steady state, whether that steady state be a constant climb or descent, or maintaining a level altitude. Once the autopilot is told what to do, it can make all those little changes without further pilot action.

ENGINE FAILURE DURING CLIMB, CRUISE, OR DESCENT

First, it is important to reemphasize how reliable turbo-fan "jet" engines are. The chances of an engine malfunction are less than one per 50,000 hours of flight. But for the sake of example, let's say an engine was to fail in cruise. With an engine shutdown, less total thrust is available, therefore the maximum cruising altitude will be lower. This lower maximum cruise altitude is called the drift down altitude. When dispatch is selecting a route, they must verify that the drift down altitude is at least 1000 feet above any terrain or obstacle. Typical drift down altitudes are 25,000 to 27,000 feet with one of two engines shut down on a twin, and two of four engines on a 747. If these altitudes seem higher than you would expect, remember, at cruise the power needed to maintain level flight is well below the power available. With one engine failed, the other can somewhat compensate.

If an engine falters in flight because of an internal part failure, there is little likelihood it can be restarted. However, if the failure was caused by a "flame-out" in the combustion section, or any other transient problem, a restart is possible. Pilots can differentiate between the two by consulting their engine windmilling charts. If the engine continues to windmill (spin) after a failure at greater than a calculated rate, the problem was not a part failure and a restart may be attempted. If a critical part has failed, the engine, in all likelihood, will not be spinning at all.

TOTAL ENGINE FAILURE

What if all the engines failed at once? It's statistically improbable, but it has happened, and the result will surprise you. Recently, a Boeing 747 had all four engines fail simultaneously when flying through some high altitude volcanic ash. The ingestion of this heavy dust caused the engines to flame out.

Though a 747 is an extremely heavy airplane, weighing up to 850,000 pounds at takeoff, it is still capable of flying like a glider. From 35,000 feet with all engines failed, the airplane is capable of gliding approximately 70 miles in any direction to a suitable landing spot. How can something so big and so heavy glide? A 747 is a large airplane, but it also has a very large wing. The amount of weight each square foot of wing has to lift is no greater than aircraft many times smaller and lighter, so it can glide just as well.

To keep an airplane flying, air must pass over and under the wings. To keep this forward movement, you either need thrust or must fly slightly downhill. If your automobile engine quits driving downhill and you put the car in neutral, you will coast until the hill levels out. Same with a plane.

In the case of this 747, they glided several minutes until they were clear of the volcanic dust that caused the problem, and restarted their engines. As a precaution, the crew landed at the nearest suitable airport for an inspection.

TOTAL HYDRAULIC FAILURE

Again, there are three or more completely redundant systems, making failure unlikely. But let's take the highly improbable, and imagine that all the systems failed at once. In the smaller type aircraft, like the 727, the backup to a total hydraulic failure are basic cables. Though additional force is required, similar to losing your power steering in your car, the plane's flight controls could be moved and normal flight maintained. On the larger aircraft, where the flight controls are quite a bit larger, a Ram Air Turbine (RAT) is installed as a backup to the multiple redundant hydraulic systems. With the loss of all hydraulics, the RAT would automatically drop from the lower fuselage, exposing a large propeller. As the plane traveled forward, the relative wind would spin the propeller, which in turn would spin a hydraulic pump, which would pressurize a reserve part of the hydraulics and allow the flight controls to be moved. Further, if the RAT did not deploy automatically, it could be lowered manually.

AIR-CONDITIONING SYSTEM FAILURE

If all your air-conditioning systems were to fail, which is highly unlikely, the outflow valve would automatically close tight. With all the air-conditioning systems failed, no new compressed and conditioned air would be entering the cabin. Since the outflow valve was also fully closed, almost no air would be escaping, so there would be plenty of breathable air.

Gradually it would get stuffy, but an emergency descent would not be required, though priority ATC handling would be requested. There would be plenty of time for a gradual descent to a lower altitude where the fresh outside breathable air could be filtered through the cabin. In all likelihood, the overhead emergency oxygen masks would never be needed, though most flight crews would deploy them to alleviate concern.

PRESSURIZATION SYSTEM FAILURE

If the entire pressurization system was to fail simultaneously—all three independent pressurization controllers at once—a rapid depressurization might not result either. Why? Without any pressurization signals, the outflow valve will independently close at a predetermined set cabin altitude, usually 11,000 feet. Then you're back to a similar condition as described above.

To get a rapid depressurization as depicted in the movies, all the outflow valve motors—both A.C. and D.C.—must fail at once with the outflow valve in the open position. A bomb puncturing the fuselage would also create a large enough hole to do the same. In such a depressurization, because of the higher pressure in the plane, inside air rushes out quickly, equalizing with the lower-pressure outside air. The equalization of pressure is over almost instantaneously. The outflow valve is located behind and below the cargo compartment, so it would be impossible to lose someone that way. During an explosion, a passenger in the immediate vicinity may not be as fortunate, but if you survive the first few seconds, stay calm, you will survive.

Airplanes are required to be able to withstand a 20-square-foot hole blown in the fuselage without the loss of structural integrity. The manufacturers routinely double that standard to 40 square feet.

The first sign of a rapid depressurization would be a loud noise. The mixing of the cold outside air with the warmer cabin air inside will cause an immediate fogging of the plane. It will clear within minutes. The plane will get chilly and your ears may pop or become blocked. The oxygen masks will drop instantly, and it is your responsibility to pull it toward you, starting the oxygen flow. If you are traveling with a child, put your own mask on first.

The cockpit crew all have special quick-donning oxygen masks that can be put on with just one hand. Within two seconds the cockpit crew will be on 100 percent oxygen, alleviating the danger of losing any cognitive abilities from lack of oxygen. In routine flight above 25,000 feet, if one pilot leaves his station, for whatever reason, the other must go on oxygen. Above 41,000 feet, as a precaution, one pilot must be on oxygen all the time.

In a rapid depressurization, after the flight crew dons their oxygen masks they will assess the situation. The most rapid emergency descent may not be warranted if there is concern for the plane's structure. An emergency will be declared with Air Traffic Control, which will provide a priority clearance to a lower altitude. Again, it may not be prudent simply to descend; verification that the altitudes below are clear of other aircraft is worth a few seconds of delay. The power will be retarded to idle. The captain will lower the aircraft's pitch attitude to between 5 and 10 degrees nose down. Doesn't sound like a great deal, but it will feel very steep. The speed brakes will be deployed to compensate for the tendency of the airplane to accelerate. The descent rate will be greater than 6000 feet per minute, the maximum we can read on our vertical speed indicators. Level off will be at 14,000 feet or below, low enough so supplemental oxygen is no longer needed. The emergency descent will be over in about three minutes, considerably less than the minimum 12 minutes of oxygen carried on board. Pilot's practice this whole procedure during recurrent training every six months.

DESCENT

Imagine there is no Air Traffic Control, no conflicting air traffic, no wind or inclement weather. If descent was taking place in a completely uncluttered environment—one free of Air Traffic Control, other planes, wind and weather—pilots would descend on a three to one line. For every three miles of distance traveled toward the destination, 1000 feet of altitude would be lost. If the plane were cruising at 35,000 feet, an ideal descent would be started no later than 105 miles from the airport. Since it is highly desirable to be smooth, an additional 15 miles would be added to the 105 miles, so a slow transition could be made from cruise to descent.

In reality, though, there are many other factors to consider. Tailwinds might make it necessary to start the descent earlier to compensate for the increased speed over the ground. Headwinds might require a later top of descent point, or a more gradual rate. ATC altitude restrictions might dictate a descent in stages, step-down clearances similar to the step climbs on the way up, with the resultant pitch and power changes. The flight may have to fly slightly out of its way to be sequenced with other arrival traffic. Flying beyond the airport and circling back to land into the wind can add 40 miles to a flight, another necessary part of the calculation.

But in general terms, most flights plan to arrive 30 miles from the destination—at 10,000 feet and already slowed to 250 knots (288 mph)—which is ideal in making a smooth transition to the approach segment.

Given ATC clearance at the calculated top of descent point, the flight crew begins a very gradual pitch down of the nose—1 or 2 degrees lower than the level cruise attitude—and the plane begins to descend. Initially, the rate of descent is only 1000 feet per minute. After four minutes—or 4000 feet, as a general rule—the descent rate will be increased. The nose of the plane will be lowered a couple of degrees further and the rate of descent increased to 2000 to 3000 feet per minute. The airplane is capable of descent rates significantly higher, and at times, because of conflicting traffic and late ATC descent clearances, higher rates are used. When ATC clears an aircraft out of its cruising altitude—usually to 24,000 feet first, and later 10,000 feet—traffic separation must be provided at every altitude the plane descends through. It would be a considerably more difficult task if it were not for the SID's and STAR's mentioned earlier. Standard Instrument Departures, and Standard Terminal Arrival Routes group, sequence and separate the inbound traffic from the outbound.

There are times when Air Traffic Control asks a plane to descend and slow down at the same time. Airplanes are designed with very little aerodynamic drag, so even with the power back to idle, it can be difficult to slow in a descent. For this purpose, speed brakes, those large panels near the trailing edge of the wing, were installed. Normally the panels are completely stowed in the zero-degree position. With a pull of the speed brake handle in the cockpit, they can be raised in any increment from zero to 40 degrees. The extra drag serves to slow the aircraft down while increasing the descent rate without further lowering the nose of the plane.

One final note about descent. Given no descent restrictions, it would be possible from just beyond the top of descent point to reduce power on all the engines to idle and glide to the destination. In fact, the most fuel-efficient descent safely incorporates idle power glides into each and every flight.

CHAPTER 12

WEATHER PHENOMENA

There is always a certain amount of water vapor in the air. When air is cooled, the water vapor is squeezed out and becomes visible as a cloud. When the weather is dry, days of low humidity, there isn't as much moisture in the air, lessening the potential for clouds. Meteorologists are able to measure the moisture content of the air and determine exactly at what temperature the air will become saturated with water vapor. That temperature is called the dewpoint. The dewpoint temperature is lower on dry days and higher on more humid days.

Since clouds restrict visibility, predicting when a clear day will get foggy is an essential part of aviation weather forecasting. If the surface temperature is 50 degrees and the dewpoint is measured to be 49, further cooling of the air will cause fog to develop. As the sun reheats the air, the fog will dissipate.

TYPES OF CLOUDS

There are two types of clouds: cumulus and stratus clouds. Cumulus are the large, fluffy, beautiful puffballs. Because convective air is needed to form cumulus clouds, flying near or in them causes a choppy ride. Stratus are flat, layered clouds, which are usually smooth to fly through.

In grade school it becomes confusing when the cumulus and stratus clouds were given prefixes of alto and cirrus. No more. If a cumulus cloud is labeled altocumulus, the alto simply defines it as a higher altitude cumulus cloud. If a cloud is labeled cirrus, it means the cloud will be found at altitudes in excess of 25,000 feet. Nimbus is added after the cloud type to indicate some intensity of precipitation. A cumulonimbus cloud is a cumulus cloud carrying rain or snow. A pilot would try to fly around this. In the daytime it's easy. At night pilots depend on their weather radar to "see" the clouds.

WEATHER RADAR

Weather radar signals are emitted from a 30-inch plate in the nose of the aircraft. It detects moisture in the air. Contrary to popular belief, radar can not see clouds, only the moisture contained within. The greater the moisture content, the easier the radar can "see the cloud."

The weather radar antenna can be tilted 15 degrees up and down and nearly 90 degrees left and right. The newer radars are capable of seeing the weather up to distances of 320 miles in front of the flight path. Weather radar is more accurate at the higher altitudes, since closer to the ground lakes, rivers, oceans, and even buildings in a downtown area can clutter the scope. Weather radar can differentiate the intensity of the rain, snow, or ice by using different shades of green on a single color radar, and by using greens, yellows, and reds on the newer color CRT screens.

TURBULENCE

Turbulence is a major concern of most passengers, particularly the fearful ones. Pilots also dislike rough air, not because of any fear of the plane being damaged, but because we know it is discomforting for the passengers. Flight crews go to great lengths to avoid turbulence, but the occasional unforecasted area of rough air is difficult to avoid. All turbulence is reported to ATC and the airline's own meteorological department to help the planes flying behind avoid the same bumps.

Turbulence is rated in terms of light, moderate, and severe. In light turbulence, passengers might feel a slight strain against their seat belts. In moderate turbulence, a definite strain will be felt. Severe turbulence can cause a more violent jarring against your seat belt and may even toss some unsecured object, like food service trays. Severe turbulence is extremely rare, and in many ways easier to forecast than lesser grades of chop. Any severe turbulence forecast will be issued and reissued as necessary in the form of a SIGMET (Significant Meteorological Condition).

Even the roughest turbulence seldom lasts a long time—a hard thing to convince passengers as they are being bumped around. Many times a change of route or altitude will lead to smooth air. Think of it like pilots do—turbulence is a tolerated nuisance. Most of the time the air is very smooth. Sometimes, like the ocean, the air can develop waves, similar to the rolling swells at sea. These swells can be small, medium, or large, but just like an oceanic cruise ship, the rocking motion doesn't upset the aircraft, it only annoys the passengers.

AIR POCKETS

Among passengers who fear turbulence, there is a common fear that a plane can be flying level at 35,000 feet and suddenly fall. To use the ocean analogy again, a cruise ship can be sailing along over swells, bobbing up and down, but regardless of the intensity, the ship never plummets to the bottom of the sea. The same holds true in the air. In choppy air the plane can be bounced around, and it can feel as if it is falling. But it isn't. People find it hard to believe that even in some of the worst turbulence, a change in altitude is hardly indicated on the altimeters.

WHAT CAUSES TURBULENCE

The cases of turbulence are many and varied. First, there is convective air, which is ordinarily responsible for the bit of choppy air when a plane is within 3000 to 4000 feet of the ground. This can be the result of the earth's rotation, which creates friction between the ground and the atmosphere and results in changing winds. Buildings and mountains near airports can also alter wind conditions, causing choppy air. And in the desert, uneven heating of the earth's surface can produce thermals, more rough air. But this, too, is often nothing more than light turbulence.

The second cause of turbulence is usually associated with clouds, air masses, and fronts—the type of weather discussed on the evening news. This is fairly predictable. Cumulus clouds can be full of bumpy air, and avoided. Whenever a weather front is crossed, flying from a warm to a cold front and vice versa, there will be a change in temperature and wind direction, and with that, possible turbulence. Before departure, the flight crew will have studied the various weather charts and determined how to avoid the fronts or cross them at their smoothest altitude and location.

During the flight, pilots look for other clues of impending choppy air. Rapid changes in the outside air temperature, changes in wind speed and/or direction, and changes in barometric pressure, can signal turbulence ahead.

CLEAR AIR TURBULENCE

Clear air turbulence (CAT) is different from the chop associated with clouds and fronts. On beautiful days, when the sky is as clear as can be, the conditions that give rise to CAT can be present. Rapid changes in pressure plotted on isobar charts, marked temperature fluctuations forecasted on isotherm charts, and dramatic changes in wind direction and velocity, especially around the boundaries of the jet stream, are all clues that clear air turbulence is a possibility. Because CAT forecasting is not yet an exact science, if any of the above conditions are present, flight crews exercise precaution and leave the seat-belt light on longer than may seem necessary.

THUNDERSTORMS AND ASSOCIATED TURBULENCE

Thunderstorms give rise to some of the worst turbulence and have to be avoided. Thunderstorms are caused by the mixing of hot and cold air that has become capable of carrying a great volume of moisture to very high altitudes. As the air is churned up and down, again and again, a thunderstorm is born. This very unstable gusty air can give rise to heavy rainshowers, hail, lightning, and tornadoes. Individually, thunderstorms can be nasty. Grouped together, they are called a squall line and even worse.

Thunderstorms have definite life cycles. They begin as lower clouds and then build into the upper atmosphere. Their tops can rise above 50,000 feet, and during the storm's building stage, some turbulence is expected, but it's the mature thunderstorm that contains the severe weather and worst turbulence. As the convective air that gave birth to the thunderstorm dissipates, so does the violent air.

A thunderstorm near the airport during takeoff is not a threat to the flight's safety. The plane will simply stay on the ground. If there's a thunderstorm over the airport during approach, the plane will simply hold a safe distance until it moves away. In cruise, during the daytime, thunderstorms are easily circumnavigated visually and by use of the weather radar. At night, pilots rely on the radar alone, but as mentioned, the heavier the storm, the better the radar picture. Above 20,000 feet the rule is to fly no closer than 20 miles to avoid the moderate and possibly severe turbulence. Flying on the upwind side of the direction of the storm's movement will provide the smoothest ride and least risk of hail. Slowing the airspeed to a predetermined turbulent speed will help smooth out the bumps if any are present, just like a car would slow on a bumpy road.

THUNDERSTORMS AND LIGHTNING

Planes are equipped with white flashing anticollision wing-tip strobe lights, which, when flying through clouds, are sometimes mistaken for lightning. There have been other times when static electricity builds on a plane and its sudden discharge is mistaken for a strike. In cruise, a plane will not fly closer than 20 miles to a thunderstorm. However, when a plane is within the vicinity, static electricity may build up on the plane, particularly on the nose, which is the area subject to the most air friction. Airplanes have static electricity wicks located on the wing tips and tail. These are points at which the static electricity is discharged. If the static electricity builds up faster than the wicks can steadily discharge it, a rapid discharge accompanied by a white flash might be seen. Anyone who has dried clothes in a dryer without using antistatic products knows about static electricity. Static electricity is not a hazard and does not affect any of the airborne equipment.

Just the word lightning sometimes evokes fear in air travelers. It shouldn't. First, an airplane is not grounded, so there is nothing to attract lightning to it. Second, lightning strikes are extremely rare and highly unlikely occurrences. In the worst-case scenario of a plane that just happened to be in the path of lightning discharging from a thunderstorm to the ground, a freak strike could occur. Since the plane's aluminum surface is a very good conductor, the electricity would quickly pass through the aircraft's skin. The only result would be a very small burn mark.

As for the various systems on the plane, they would be unaffected. The hydraulic system would not be damaged by a lightning strike, nor the electrical system, which is insulated by surge protectors. The fuel system is usually the passengers' biggest concern, and the possibility exists that lightning could put a tiny pinhole in the wing, and then fuel could very slowly drip out. The chance of this occurring is minute, and even in the worst-case possibility, a divert to a nearby airport is always an alternative. The hazard of a fire or explosion is statistically nil. Jet fuel, stored in the tanks, is not very flammable. It needs to be vaporized, heated to greater than 100 degrees, and mixed with oxygen to burn. A lightning strike would be scary, but it would not be dangerous.

HAIL

Hail is a hazard associated with thunderstorms, and every effort will be made to avoid it. The concern isn't so much for structural damage as it is for the havoc hail might play with the outside paint job. Most hail is found between the months of April and June, and usually between two and ten P.M. The most severe hail often falls between the Continental Divide in the Rockies and the Mississippi River. Since hail is fairly short-lived, and falls in a narrow band, if a plane gets caught in a hailstorm, the pilot is apt to just push ahead and get it over with quickly rather than turn around and, perhaps, prolong the battering.

ICE

Passengers are often concerned about the buildup of ice on the wings. A buildup could disrupt the airflow over and under the wing, reducing the lift capability and adding excess weight. But ice in cruise is not as great a hazard as perceived. When the outside air is a little above 32 degrees Fahrenheit (zero degrees Celsius), the precipitation is rain. Several degrees below the freezing temperature the precipitation is already frozen as snow. Ice can only form on an aircraft if rain freezes on contact. Since the atmosphere gets colder the higher a plane climbs, there is only a small altitude range where the outside air temperature is actually at freezing. This altitude is called the freezing level. When operating near this freezing level with visible moisture present, the engine and wing anti-ice will be turned on to heat up the critical surfaces and prevent any ice buildup. In the very remote worst-case scenario, with the entire system inoperative and ice accumulating on the plane, a change in altitude away from this freezing level would provide a solution.

CONTRAILS

Nearly everyone has at one time or another looked up in the sky and noticed long white streaks trailing behind a high flying jet. Some last a few minutes, some a long time. These white streaks are called contrails. They are formed when heated hydrogen, a by-product of burned jet fuel, mixes with the atmospheric oxygen to make water. If the temperature is cold enough, the water will immediately freeze into ice crystals. These tiny ice crystals are what you actually see.

Severe weather can be frightening. Despite the fact that airplanes are constructed with the worst weather in mind, pilots develop a healthy respect for the weather from their very first flight. While it is not possible to avoid every little inconsequential bump, every effort is made to steer clear of all significant weather. One of the great advantages of air travel is that circumnavigating bad weather, even when it means flying 100 miles or more off course, adds only minutes to a passenger's flight time.

CHAPTER 13

APPROACH TO LAND

The approach phase of the flight begins long before the plane is actually lined up with the runway to land. Twenty to 40 miles from your destination, the en route ATC center will clear you into the approach area. ATC approach control then becomes responsible for traffic separation and aircraft sequencing. At major airports with heavy traffic volume, approach control is divided into sectors with distinct radio frequencies.

RUNWAYS

Landing requires less distance than takeoff, so it's possible to land at an airport that you can't later depart from. Most runways in the United States are 8000 to 10,000 feet long—almost two miles. With a maximum effort, most planes could be stopped in 2500 feet, but that would be uncomfortable and cause a great deal of brake and tire wear. Airlines use approximately 5500 feet as a minimum.

In cruise—or in the early part of the descent—planning for approach begins. Similar to takeoff, a thorough review must be made to verify that the flight crew, airplane, and airport all meet the minimum standards to begin the approach.

For the first 100 to 300 hours, new captains—either first-time captains or just new to an airplane—must observe higher than standard approach minimums. This term, "minimums," means the lowest altitude a pilot can descend without having visual contact with the runway. On average, minimum altitudes are raised 100 feet and the minimum visibility requirement one-half mile for the pilot new in the "left seat." The fact that the captain may have flown thousands of hours as a co-pilot on this very plane does not count. High minimums still apply.

The airplane must also be legal. If something has malfunctioned in flight, depending on the type of problem, better weather will be required before the plane is cleared to approach at the lowest minimums. The runway has to be long enough. Of course, you will never be dispatched to an airport with a runway too short to accommodate your flight. A runway is considered long enough if the plane can come to a complete stop in 60 percent of the total length after touching down 1000 feet from the runway threshold (beginning).

What if during flight one of the brakes or antiskid systems developed a problem? Naturally, the stopping capability of the plane is reduced, which would require a longer runway. Consulting an Aircraft Restrictions Manual (ARM), which is carried in every cockpit, the pilot can discern if the 40 percent margin of error is still met. The use of reverse thrust after landing is never calculated into the landing figures.

RUNWAY CONDITIONS

Stopping capability can also be affected by the condition of the runway itself. As noted earlier, runways are grooved and crowned—grooved to provide rapid drainage, and crowned in the center to direct water off to the sides. Still, wet runways can be slippery. Whenever the runway is reported wet, or the visibility goes below three-quarters of a mile—there's moisture in the air—15 percent has to be added to the minimum runway length. Above one-half inch of water on the runway and a landing would be illegal. Snow on the runway also requires extra approach planning. Wet slushy snow has similar limits as standing water. Dry snow provides more friction for stopping than wet snow, so a slightly greater accumulation is allowed. However, if the stopping ability ever gets below a certain level as determined by an airport vehicle designed to measure braking coefficients, or as reported by a flight crew, the runway has to be plowed. Runways are routinely plowed long before they ever get to that point.

Other situations can also cause a runway to be too short to land. If another plane becomes disabled on the runway, it will have to be closed. If maintenance is required, then that portion of the runway will have to be closed.

AIRPORT WEATHER

Near the top of descent the pilots listen to the arrival ATIS (Automatic Terminal Information Service). The arrival ATIS provides weather for the current destination and the active runways. It's updated every hour, or as conditions change. Included in the broadcast are:

1. Cloud coverage and how low to the ground they are, so pilots know what to expect when they "break out"
2. Visibility, so they know how far they should be able to see when they do "break out"
3. The kind and extent of any precipitation, so pilots know the reason for the visibility restrictions
4. The temperature (Could the precipitation freeze? Do they need engine and wing anti-ice?)
5. The dewpoint, in order to discern the possibility of fog

6. The wind direction and velocity—calm or gusty, straight down the runway or a crosswind
7. The barometric altimeter setting, to recalibrate altimeters for current height above sea level
8. The active runways and the type of instrument procedure used to navigate to that runway
9. Any special situations, including the field conditions, braking action, RVR (runway visual range), the actual visibility as measured by a machine (transmissometer) located at the runway, forecast or reported windshear, runway cutback, taxiway closed, lights inoperative, or anything else pertinent

APPROACH PLANNING

Among the items on the ATIS tape is a description of the active runway and the instrument approach available to use. Many runways have more than one type of electronic guidance system to align you with the runway when visibility is poor. All pilot flight kits contain a complete set of manuals depicting the approach procedure for every airport served by that airline, plus all the alternate airports. Each approach chart for the airport is labeled by name, numbered, and dated. Once the type of approach and runway have been assigned, a thorough review of the procedure takes place.

First you verify the correct approach plate. With numerous parallel runways, it would be a grand mistake to confuse 27R (right) with 27L (left). Each approach has a specific navigational aid with its own distinct frequency which must be tuned and identified. Morse code transmitted over this special frequency is still used for positive identification. The inbound magnetic course must be set. For example, a runway named Runway 27 faces roughly 270 degrees, which is west on the compass. Since runway names are rounded to the nearest 10 degrees, Runway 27's direction could be anywhere from 265 to 275 degrees. However, on an approach, we want to be accurate to the nearest degree, so the approach chart tells us the exact magnetic direction of the runway. If it's 272 degrees, we set 272.

Crossing altitudes must be reviewed. The approach chart tells you exactly what altitude you should be at any specific point. Also the lowest minimum altitude you can descend, without visual reference to the runway, must be determined. The approach chart highlights the standard minimum altitudes with everything operating, as well as more restrictive higher minimum altitudes if any of the ground-based equipment or airport lighting is not operating. The pilots determine which minimums apply.

Just like almost everything else, pilots always plan for "what if" situations. The "missed approach procedure" is for the rare time when you don't have visual contact with the runway at the decision height and must go-around. One hundred feet off the ground with no forward visibility is no time to be deciding which way to fly. The approach chart also highlights any special terrain features and so will guide you away from any menacing terrain. Finally, after the approach briefing is completed by the pilots, a written approach checklist is read to verify that all items have been completed.

APPROACH SEQUENCING

Through the approach preparation and briefing, the plane is still flying toward the airport. The actual airspeed of the plane may be slowing down, but the pace of the pilot's job is increasing. Descending through 10,000 feet, the ATC speed limit must be observed; the plane will be slowed to 250 knots. The Sterile Cockpit Rule applies as it did on initial climb, so only announcements relating to the safety of flight can be made by the pilots. No more sightseeing announcements.

At busy airports it's rare to be cleared straight into the runway. Some form of approach sequencing usually takes place. Initially, ATC will request a speed adjustment to increase the spacing between inbound traffic. The lead airplanes fly faster and the trailers slow down. Since approach control has to sequence traffic from all directions, not just the arrival route you are flying, additional spacing may be required.

This is where vectors are used. Vectors are turns issued by ATC off the published arrival route. A couple of turns left and right may adjust the traffic pattern perfectly. However, if ATC becomes saturated with inbound traffic and has no airspace closer to the airport available for your flight, a holding will be issued. A holding pattern is essentially an oval orbit in the sky. If a holding is issued, the plane flies to a clearance limit point, called the holding fix, and makes right or left turns in the sky. The pattern is oval so not as many turns have to be made. When weather closes an airport temporarily, planes sometimes get "stacked up" in a holding pattern. What this means is that more than one airplane is holding at the same fix, but never at altitudes closer than 1000 feet.

During approach delays, a satisfying announcement to passengers is hard to make. Pilots are acutely aware that many passengers have connecting flights to catch. They are also sensitive that the approach Air Traffic Controller is very busy and does not have time to talk with the other approach controller working the other inbound sectors to determine your exact sequence. Approach does issue an "expect further clearance" or "expect approach clearance" time, but that can change. Delays are a nuisance, an inconvenience to the passenger, and an added expense to the airline. But safety can make them unavoidable.

INSTRUMENT LANDING SYSTEM APPROACH (ILS)

The primary approach at most airports uses the Instrument Landing System. An ILS transmitter, located at the runway, sends signals that are received by the multiple ILS receivers on board. Actually, it sends two separate and distinct signals. A localizer signal is transmitted in a narrow horizontal beam 6 degrees wide, and lets you know if you are right, left, or directly on course. A glide slope beam 1.4 degrees vertical tells you if you are on the correct slope to the runway. Normal glide slopes are angles at 3 degrees, requiring 300 feet of altitude to be lost every mile on the approach, or approximately 700 feet per minute. Not very steep.

Two needles are displayed on the flight instruments. If the localizer needle is exactly centered, the airplane will be directly in line with the runway center line. Any time the needle moves from that perfect center position, a slight turn is needed to correct back to course. There are dots on the localizer scale. Each dot on the instrument represents one degree. If the needle moves one dot, you're one degree off. More than 2 degrees will cause full-scale needle deflection. One-half dot off course, with weather near minimums, is reason enough to initiate a go-around, even though one-half dot is only 175 feet off course.

The glide slope is like the localizer, but turned on its side and four times more precise. Being just 14 feet high or low over the runway will cause a full-scale needle deflection. Part of its precision is due to the location of the transmitters. The glide slope transmitter is only 1000 feet beyond the runway threshold. Because it's providing only vertical guidance, it does not have to be on the runway—only aligned with the touchdown aim point. The localizer antenna, on the other hand, must be perfectly aligned with the runway center line, which is why it's located at the far end of the runway—up to two miles away.

A complete ILS system has many other necessary components, including altitude marker beacons, lights, and runway markings. A high intensity approach lighting system begins more than a half mile from the threshold. Sequence flashers and white strobe lights that flash in rapidfire succession toward the runway provide visual lead-in guidance for runway alignment. These sequence flashers are commonly called "the rabbit," because of the hop, hop, hop visual effect. Runway end identifier lights—which actually mark the beginning—runway edge lights, runway center-line lights, and runway touchdown zone lights, all highlight the exact dimensions of the runway.

The touchdown aim point is 1000 feet from the thresh-old. If you aimed for the very beginning of the runway, there would be no margin of error for landing short. A 3000-foot touchdown zone is highlighted with lights and big heavy white lines painted on the cement. If a touch-down can't be made in the touchdown zone, a go-around will be made. Runway remaining lights use colors to indicate how much runway is left. At 3000 feet, white and red; at 2000 feet it's amber; the final 1000 feet is all red.

DIFFERENT GRADES OF INSTRUMENT LANDING SYSTEM (ILS) APPROACHES

ILS approaches are divided into three categories: CAT I, CAT II, and CAT III. CAT I approaches allow a descent to a minimum-decision-height altitude of 200 feet above ground level and a landing with 1800 feet forward visibility as measured by the RVR (runway visual range) meter. CAT II minimums are a decision height of 100 feet AGL and 1200 feet RVR. CAT III is the epitome of a high technology approach. No decision height is stipulated because a full autopilot-autoland system is required and used to land the plane. Visibility is required to be 700 feet RVR (soon to be lowered to 300 feet), but very little if any of the runway will be seen by the pilots before touchdown. Why the difference in visibility? The airport itself must adhere to higher standards to receive and maintain CAT II and CAT III certification. For the airlines to use this capability, their airplanes must be equipped and maintained to higher standards, and their pilots specifically trained in these extremely low-visibility landing procedures. What this means to the passengers is that some pilots and planes can land in denser fog than others.

VISUAL APPROACH

The other common instrument approach is a visual approach. Using instrument and visual together may seem like a contradiction, but a visual approach is an instrument procedure. Radar coverage, electronic approach guidance, and full localizer and glide slope information are all still used. But when the visibility is good, pilots can also see the runway and other aircraft from long distances. Spacing between airplanes can be safely decreased using "visuals." For example, on parallel runways closer together than 4300 feet, aircraft cannot fly the approach side by side when the visibility is restricted. When the visibility is greater than three miles, this restriction no longer applies.

Visual approaches are also used for noise abatement procedures. Landing to the south at Washington National, for example, a Potomac River noise abatement visual is common. By flying the entire approach over the river, noise from the aircraft can be minimized on the ground. Pitch and power changes will be frequent, and multiple turns will have to be made at low altitude. LaGuardia Airport in New York has a similar noise abatement visual approach procedure. Arriving from the south, the pilots are required to fly over the Long Island Expressway until turning for Runway 31. San Francisco has the Quiet Bridge and Tipp Toe visual approaches. Flying over the San Francisco Bay until runway alignment is needed for landing is a good-neighbor policy. Other airports have similar noise abatement procedures.

Weather permitting, some airports use visual approaches as part of the "keep them high" noise abatement policy. Aircraft regularly are required to maintain altitudes above the normal 3 degree descent path. Once given approach clearance, a steeper than normal descent rate will be used to reintercept the normal slope. The intercept will always occur a safe distance from the runway. The higher altitude limits the noise that can be heard on the ground. The steeper rate reduces the power requirement. Visual approaches, with or without noise abatement procedures, are never issued when weather is a factor.

FLYING THE APPROACH

Within 10 to 20 miles of the airport the aircraft will gradually be slowed to the minimum flaps up "clean speed"—usually 210 to 230 knots (242 to 265 mph). The flight attendants will be signaled that the plane is five to ten minutes from landing, which gives them time to complete their FAA-required duties and be seated themselves. All seat backs must be upright, the tray tables and any carry-on luggage properly stowed, and if a smoking flight, all cigarettes extinguished. Entering the airport traffic pattern downwind, the flaps and slats will begin to be lowered in increments. For example, on the 767 the flaps have flap settings of 1, 5, 15, 20, 25, and 30 degrees. The slats are extended as a function of flap position. Flap and slat activation can be noisy. With the flaps and slats partially or fully extended, a vibration can also be felt from the additional aerodynamic drag.

Each flap position has a maximum and minimum speed. The maximum speed is fixed, a never-exceed structural limit speed for each degree of extension. The minimum speeds for each position are calculated by the flight crew to always provide the 30 percent margin above stall speed. Typical minimum speeds are 180 knots (207 mph) for flaps 5 degrees; 160 knots (184 mph) for flaps 15; 140 knots (161 mph) for flaps 20; and a final approach speed for full flaps of 130 to 135 knots (150 to 155 mph). These are the minimums. Many times the airspeeds will be higher. The first several flap positions, combined with slat extension, do the most to increase the lifting capability of the wing. Additional flap extension predominately increases the drag.

Approximately five to seven miles from the runway, the landing gear is lowered. Similar to takeoff, after the landing gear goes down, the gear doors are closed again. The landing gear is a very high-drag item. An earlier than normal extension can help to increase the descent rate without increasing the airspeed. The gear will be down and locked a minimum of three miles from touchdown, 1000 feet above the ground. The flaps will be in the landing position, the airspeed slowed to the final approach speed, and the before-landing checklist completed to verify everything is done.

WAKE TURBULENCE

After a smooth flight, it's disappointing to have less than a perfectly smooth approach. However, just like the takeoff and initial climb, the plane on approach is back to a lower-altitude environment, where convective air can cause gusty winds and low-level chop. Also, with flaps extended the outboard ailerons—most larger planes have two sets— are active, and an increase in the roll sensitivity can sometimes be felt. Also, the flying has to be more precise on approach. Being a few feet off in cruise is insignificant. But now the pilots are constantly making small adjustments to stay exactly on course. Most of these are expected and understood by the passengers.

What usually gives rise to most concern during approach is wake turbulence—also called wing-tip vortices. As discussed in aerodynamics, the high pressure below the wing and the low pressure on top is the fundamental reason for lift. Around the wing tip the only place where the air can swirl from the bottom to the top is where the two differential pressures try to equalize. This circular motion can develop tremendous speed and temporarily upset the air even on a smooth, calm day. Think of the motorboat analogy. Take a boat on a lake that's perfectly calm, and as you speed through the water, a sizable wake is created. After a few moments the water returns to its original calm.

Wake turbulence created by the wings of the airplane is similar, except that pilots can't see it. Since the wake of a plane has a tendency to descend as well as dissipate rapidly, being behind another aircraft at the same altitude should not cause a bumpy ride. Approach control spaces aircraft so they will never fly too close to the wake of the plane in front. Normal separation is a minimum of three miles, which is increased to a minimum of five miles if you are following a heavy jumbo jet.

However, wake turbulence can be blown laterally in a crosswind as it is descending. There are times, no matter the extent of the precautions, when you will inadvertently fly through another aircraft's wake turbulence. The circular motion of the wake causes a rolling motion of the plane. It's felt as a sudden jolt and is over almost instantly. Wake turbulence is usually unexplained by the flight crew because of the Sterile Cockpit Rule.

WINDSHEAR

Windshear is a rapid change of wind speed and/or direction over a very short distance. Windshear can be found at any altitude, but only near the ground does it become a concern. A vertical windshear, called a microburst, is the most hazardous because the downdraft can be severe. Picture a bucket of water being poured onto your driveway. The water falls straight down, but upon hitting the ground, much of it splashes outward and upward.

What happens? When you approach the runway, you first encounter the updraft—the water from the bucket being splashed back up—and the airplane has a tendency to rise. The indicated airspeed also increases because of the rapidly increasing headwind—the water being splashed to the side. To an unsuspecting pilot, the tendency would be to lower the nose to reestablish the glide slope and to reduce the power to slow down. A split second later, you fly into the core of the downdraft—the water being poured from the bucket. The airspeed drops and the rate of descent increases. The power must be rapidly reapplied and a climb initiated to counter the effect of the downburst. Like the bucket of water, the column of descending air is very small, isolated and short-lived. Moments after encountering a downburst, the incident will be over.

Avoidance is the safest way of dealing with a microburst. Major airports have Low Level Windshear Alert Systems (LLWAS) which measure the wind direction and velocity at numerous locations near the airport. Conflicting readings at different locations can indicate a shear, and the tower will issue a warning. Currently, this LLWAS is being expanded to include more wind reporting locations farther outside the airport boundary. Since microbursts can be very isolated, off-airport sites are essential. A new Doppler Radar system that can locate and measure the intensity of windshear and microbursts is also being tested.

For sake of example, take a worst-case scenario. No suspicious weather, and no ground-based warnings. A plane is established on its final approach, stabilized, and descending through 1000 feet. Any time the flight path becomes somewhat unstable—the airspeed fluctuates plus or minus 15 knots, the vertical speed changes plus or minus 500 feet per minute, the pitch attitude goes up or down 5 degrees, an unusual amount of power is required to fly the approach, or you are off the glide slope by one degree—a microburst must be suspected and a windshear recovery initiated. Airplanes are capable of climb rates of 3000 and 4000 feet a minute, so the quicker the recovery is begun, the better.

New and in-service aircraft are now being fitted with a new windshear detection system. When the onboard windshear computer senses a windshear, an alert—both visually on the flight instruments and aurally using a computer-generated voice saying "Windshear, windshear" —will alarm, and windshear recovery will be started immediately.

NAVIGATION EQUIPMENT FAILURE AND NO-GYRO APPROACHES

If during the flight all navigation equipment happened to fail—the multiple ILS's, multiple VOR's, multiple NDB's, everything—the logical alternative is to proceed to an airport where the weather is good. ATC can give radar vectors to whatever airport is determined to be the best alternative. If the weather is bad at all the surrounding airfields, and an instrument approach is necessary to find the runway through the clouds, options still exist. If all your flight instruments are working and the problem is only one of navigation, an ASR (Airport Surveillance Radar), or a PAR (Precision Approach Radar), can be used. At civilian airports, approach control can guide you nearly all the way to the runway with precise radar vectors. At military airports, always available to commercial aircraft in an emergency, a PAR approach is available. A PAR approach is the military equivalent of an ILS, but no airborne equipment is required. A military ATC specialist can give you extremely accurate headings—within one degree— and glide slope guidance to the runway by using his specialized radar.

Should all flight instruments—the captain's, co-pilot's, and all the standby be inaccurate—a no-gyroscope approach can be made. Instead of issuing specific headings, the radar controller commands "turn, and stop turn." Rudimentary, but available as an emergency alternative.

CAN'T GET THE LANDING GEAR DOWN

Landing gear that can't be lowered is of great concern to many passengers. Hydraulic pressure is used to raise the landing gear into their respective wheel wells. Once completely raised and the gear doors shut, the gear is mechanically locked in the up position. On some aircraft the gear itself is locked, on others the gear simply rests on the locked gear door. After being mechanically locked, the hydraulic pressure is no longer needed and turned off.

Hydraulic pressure is normally used to lower the gear back into the down and locked position. But suppose the primary system fails to operate? The landing gear is quite heavy and massive. If you were able to release the up locks, gravity would do the rest of the job for you. Installed on all aircraft are secondary landing-gear extension systems that use either cables or electrical motors to release those locks. But if all the gear still failed to lock in the down position, there are flight maneuvers that can be used to force them down.

In the worst-case scenario, you can safely land on the usable gear, or with the gear completely up, with very little damage to the airplane—and more important, with no injuries. Airplanes that have to land with one or more gear failed have been repaired, inspected, and returned to service in less than 48 hours.

CHAPTER 14

LANDING AND TAXI IN

Landing a big modern jetliner is no piece of cake. Landings are difficult because of the precision required and the pilot's own expectations. Where an inch or two is unimportant in cruise, it can be the difference between a smooth landing and a bumpy one. Furthermore, no matter how perfect the rest of the flight, from preflight, takeoff, climb, cruise, and descent, most people's opinion of a flight is heavily swayed by the touchdown. Pilots like making a "grease job" as much as any passenger, but overemphasizing smoothness is not always the safest way to land.

STANDARD CALLOUTS

The surest way to make a good landing is to make a good approach. Having everything stabilized and "in the slot" while descending on a final approach is a must. Gear down, flaps down, on course, on speed, tower clearance to land, before landing checklist complete. At 1000 feet above the ground, flying at 140 knots (161 mph), you are a little over a minute from touchdown.

Passengers can tell they are at 1000 feet above landing by the addition of power. If you have been flying with the engines at or near idle, they need to be "spooled up." Turbofan engines are slow to accelerate. To be sure that instantaneous power is available, the thrust levers are increased from the flight idle position. Frequent small power adjustments can be heard to maintain the exact predetermined approach "bug" speed. Too slow is unacceptable. Too fast and you will use additional runway. If any deviations are observed, the pilot not flying will call them out.

In low visibility the transition from flying solely by instruments to making a visual landing is difficult. On an instrument approach it is the responsibility of one pilot to stay solely on the gauges. The ILS instruments are so sensitive that a descent below the glide slope will first be noticed electronically. Two hundred feet above the lowest altitude you can descend for the approach, the pilot not flying calls out, "Two hundred above, no flags"—meaning no malfunctions. Next he calls out, "One hundred above, no flags." "Decision height," is announced, and the pilot flying states either "Runway in sight" or "Go-around."

DECISION HEIGHT—MINIMUM DESCENT ALTITUDE

At the decision height (DH) for an ILS approach, or the minimum descent altitude (MDA) for an approach without an electronic glide slope, the decision has to be made whether to descend to the runway or go-around. The criteria is simple. Do you see the runway? Are you in position to land? Yes to both, and you can continue lower.

At this point you are cleared to land, but not committed to do so. Cleared to land means you temporarily own the runway. Whether or not you use it is ultimately up to the pilots. If you were slightly high, and concerned whether you would land in the touchdown zone, the safest alternative would be to go-around. The control tower can also rescind a landing clearance at any time. If the plane ahead was slow to exit the runway, the control tower would be required to issue a go-around. Even though the plane has flown below the decision height, it's not yet committed to land.

Surprisingly, once touched down on the runway, the plane is still not committed to land. Any time before the pilot deploys the spoilers and selects reverse thrust, a go-around is possible. In fact there is a training maneuver called a "touch and go," where you purposely touch down, roll for a short distance down the runway, and take off once again.

GO-AROUND/MISSED APPROACH

The terms go-around and missed approach are synonymous. There are many misconceptions about a go-around. Some feel it is an emergency procedure. It is not. Others think the pilots must have made an error and need another chance. No again.

The most common reason for a go-around is that the plane that proceeded you to the runway was slow in clearing. Since two aircraft cannot be on the runway at the same time, your landing clearance is withdrawn. If two aircraft begin getting closer than is normal on the approach, ATC will first ask the second aircraft to slow to his minimum speed earlier than normal. This should increase the separation. If not, ATC will alert you to the possibility of a go-around, but still let you continue. ATC is aware that low altitude go-arounds, though rare, are not dangerous. Go-arounds are time consuming for the passengers and expensive for the airline. Once around the pattern can cost upward of $500. Letting you continue in the expectation the first airplane will make the early exit can save time and expense without sacrificing safety. Of course, if the first plane is not able to make the first turnoff, then a go-around is mandatory.

Whether begun at 50 or 500 feet, the procedure is exactly the same. In fact, it takes less power to make a go-around than to make the initial takeoff. You are already at flying speed. The only requirement is to stop the descent and begin a climb. The descent rate is only about 700 feet a minute, much less than the 2000 to 3000 feet a minute at altitude. The climb rate will be better than the rate at takeoff because the plane weighs less. Think of a go-around as an extra takeoff.

An additional reason for a go-around—besides not enough visibility, an unstable approach below 1000 feet, or someone still on the runway—might be an unprepared cabin. Twenty minutes from touchdown the flight attendants are signaled by the seat-belt light to discontinue cabin service. If all the galley equipment is not stowed and passengers not buckled in, the regulations require a go-around. Go-arounds have been made because passengers refuse to come out of the bathrooms and return to their seats. Also, a problem on short final makes a missed approach likely. Short final is no time to be troubleshooting. Let's say a landing gear unsafe light is flickering, or both bulbs have simultaneously burned out. There's no risk in the air. So a go-around, a simple maneuver, is initiated, and the problem investigated where the plane is in its element.

A plane is handed off from the approach control to the tower control frequency about five to seven miles from touchdown. If in that two- to three-minute time frame the tower fails to issue a landing clearance, no matter how clear the runway looks, a go-around is also mandatory. In the remote case of a radio failure, the control tower can issue a landing clearance with color-coded light signals. Steady green and you are cleared to land. Fortunately, this good idea rarely has to be used.

THE LANDING

Large white rectangular boxes are painted on the runway on both the right and left sides. Located 1000 feet from the threshold, these mark the touchdown aim point. If you are flying an electronic glide slope, this is also the point where it intercepts the runway. The pilots sit in a cockpit up to two-thirds of a football field in front of the tail. They aim for the runway from their vantage point. If from their perspective they touch down exactly abeam the 1000-foot marker, the main landing gear will be safely on the runway. Aiming for the very beginning of the runway would not allow any margin of safety for landing short. From your window seat you can tell that the plane passes over the beginning of the runway while still 35 to 50 feet in the air. It's not high. This is by design.

Just after passing the threshold, the "flare" begins. The flare is the round-out portion of the landing where the descent rate is decreased from 700 feet per minute to very nearly zero at touchdown. That's the goal, at least. As you flare, the nose is raised farther than its nose-up pitch on the approach. Increasing the pitch increases the lift and slows the descent. At the same time, the power is reduced to idle. The airspeed over the "numbers"—the runway identification numbers painted just past the threshold—was a minimum of 30 percent over stall speed. In the flare, extra power this close to the runway translates to additional runway needed. There are times when you will hear the power increase fairly rapidly just prior to touchdown, and then pulled to idle. There are two ways to stop your descent rate. The first is raising the nose. The second is an increase in power. Many times they are used in conjunction. Airplanes are built to withstand a maximum landing rate of 600 feet per minute. At first that doesn't sound like a lot, but it is nearly equivalent to a static drop of 10 feet. Since the plane is moving forward, its downward force is never completely vertical, leaving a huge margin of safety for the occasional "firm" arrival.

The last few feet before touchdown requires excellent depth perception. At the controls of a 767, the crew is nearly 36 feet in the air when the main gear touches down. Experience helps learn the touchdown "picture." Just like parallel parking your car, the second time is easier. To help the pilots learn the correct perception, the two radio altimeters can be used for guidance. The new ones read to the nearest two feet, but a slightly miscalibrated radio altimeter would make a poor excuse for a hard landing. Landings during the day are easier. At night, and during restricted visibility, you draw more from experience.

TOUCHDOWN

Touchdown occurs first on the main gear. The last several inches makes all the difference between a "grease job" and an "arrival." Given a runway of infinite length, a grease job could be accomplished nearly every time. The power would be reduced very slowly, the pitch adjusted in minute increments as you inched your way down step by step.

But such infinite runways do not exist. Since runway length is a consideration, you try for the perfect touchdown, but you don't waste excess runway doing so. Floating beyond the touchdown zone is not calculated in the landing distance figures. Passengers do not always appreciate a firm arrival, but there are times that it is the correct way to land. If a runway is wet and/or slippery, the quicker you land, the faster you can begin to stop. Gusty wind conditions sometimes necessitate "putting it on." Foggy conditions, where the other end of the runway is not visible, lends itself to touching down with a minimum of fuss. Or if the plane behind you is a little too close, ATC might request "minimum time on the runway" to prevent his go-around.

After the main gear touches, the spoilers are deployed. Those over wing panels do what their name implies—spoil the lift. The approach speed was 30 percent over stall, so even after touchdown there is still enough speed to fly. In fact, some planes do. Aircraft with a manual spoiler extension can skip on landing. The touchdown is smooth, but this extra available lift can cause a slight bounce back into the air. Automatic spoilers remove this possibility. On main gear touchdown, the panels are automatically raised, dumping all this excess lift. The downside is that the panels can dump the lift so quickly, a smooth touchdown can be made firm as the landing gear struts are rapidly compressed.

After main gear touchdown, the nose gear is lowered to the runway. A smooth landing of the nose wheel is desired also, but similar to the main gear, there are times that this is not possible.

CROSSWIND LANDINGS

It is desirable to land an aircraft as directly into a headwind as possible. Touchdown with an airspeed of 130 knots into a 10 knot headwind means the ground speed is 120 knots. This 10 knot reduction in ground speed translates into a shorter landing roll after landing. Landing under opposite conditions would mean a 10 knot tailwind, increasing the ground speed and increasing the landing distance required. To ensure that your landing performance figures are accurate, a maximum 10 knot tailwind limit is imposed.

Most of the times a tailwind is not a factor. A tailwind landing one way is a headwind landing the other way. Tailwinds become a factor at noise-sensitive airports. After midnight at Los Angeles International Airport, all arrivals approach over the Pacific and land east. Normally, the prevailing winds are from the ocean, so a tailwind can be expected when the winds are not calm. If the tailwind limit is exceeded, the "airport must be turned around." It's not the most desirable situation for the airport's neighbors, but it's a legal responsibility.

Most of the time the wind is not straight down the runway, so a crosswind component figure is calculated. Actual winds are given on the ATIS weather tape, and by the control tower. Taking the actual wind, we can determine how much of the wind is acting as headwind and how much as a 90 degree right or left crosswind. If a wind was reported 45 degrees off our right at 20 knots, the headwind would be half, 10 knots, and the direct crosswind component the same 10 knots. (The math is only this simple with a zero, 45, and 90 degree wind).

Landing in a crosswind is different than landing into a headwind. All commercial aircraft must be able to land with a crosswind component of at least 25 knots. Most are certified with 29 to 39 knot, direct 90 degree crosswind limits. During the approach, the plane will be level, but the nose will not be directly aimed at the runway. Aiming the nose upstream, toward the crosswind, will maintain a path over the ground straight to the runway. This is no different than boating with a water current from the side. This crabbing—from the ground it looks like you're flying sideways—can be adjusted to take the plane precisely to the runway threshold, just as in a headwind.

However, the touchdown technique changes because of a crosswind. If this crabbing technique were carried out all the way to the runway, the aircraft would land directly on the runway center but cocked off to the side. This would put a great deal of sideways stress on the landing gear. Instead, just before touchdown, the plane is banked into the wind and the nose held straight with the rudder. What's uniquely different is that because the airplane is in a slight bank at touchdown, the upwind landing gear will land first and be closely followed by the other main gear and then the nose wheel. This is a normal crosswind landing. Because one main gear touches down first, the automatic spoiler deployment may cause the other main gear to be firmly planted on the ground. Again, perfectly smooth does not mean perfectly safe.

AUTOLAND/AUTOTHROTTLE

When correctly programmed, the high technology aircraft are capable of landing themselves. When the visibility gets below 1200 feet RVR—about a quarter of a mile—use of this autoland and autothrottle capability is required. On an autoland approach, three independent autopilots are working side by side in a fail operational mode. All three autopilots "talk" with each other and compare data. If the computers detect a malfunction with one autopilot, the other two can do the job. Loss of two autopilots is said to make the system fail-passive, and autoland capability is lost.

The autopilots fly the ILS localizer and glide slope. Descending through 1500 feet, a flare and roll-out mode is armed. An autopilot status display in front of both pilots clearly annunciates the condition of the complete autopilot system. Any flags, and a go-around will be made.

Because the legal visibility required is soon to be as low as 300 feet, the pilots may not see the runway before touchdown. An alert height at 50 feet above the ground serves as a "check all systems" altitude. Descending through 45 to 25 feet, the autopilots begin a gradual flare, and begin to retard the power just as if the pilots were flying. Up until five feet above the ground, when the roll-out mode is captured, a go-around can still be made. Of course, a go-around made at that altitude may involve runway contact, but the gear is down so runway contact is not a problem.

After landing, the auto roll-out feature continues to track the localizer—remember, the antenna is located off the far end of the runway—until you come to a complete stop on the runway. Most autoland aircraft have autobrakes also, which are set by the pilots for a specific deceleration rate. After coming to a complete stop, the autopilot is disconnected and the airplane taxies clear of the runway. Autolands have their greatest value when it is foggy and the visibility extremely limited. However, the autoland capability can be used in good weather, for two important reasons. First, by regulation, the system must be tested at regular intervals or it loses its autoland certification. Second, even though the pilots practice autoland approaches and very low altitude go-arounds during recurrent training, real airplane practice increases confidence in the system for when it's really needed. Except for an announcement, passengers have no way of knowing if the plane was manually or automatically landed.

STOPPING THE AIRCRAFT

The basic way to stop an airplane is with the brakes. Multiple disc brakes are located on each main gear tire. Earlier models are made of steel, the latest design is a carbon brake. Widebody aircraft are capable of absorbing well over 60 million foot-pounds of energy, the equivalent stopping power of 6000 family cars. The brake pedals are actually the upper portion of the rudder pedals. The pedal pressure required is only slightly more than your automobile. Light to moderate braking is normally all that is required. Heavy or maximum braking is only used in emergencies and is capable of stopping the airplane in less than 2500 feet. The antiskid system allows the pilot to apply brake pressure, while the system itself applies and releases the brakes as necessary to prevent a skid on slippery runways. Newer aircraft have the traditional manual brakes and an automatic braking system that allows the pilots to preselect a certain after-landing deceleration rate. The rate can be changed during the roll-out.

Reverse engine thrust is also used to slow the aircraft after landing. Just after touchdown, a second set of thrust levers attached to the principal throttles are used to select reverse thrust. A common misconception about reverse thrust is that the engines turn in the opposite direction during its use. Actually, during reverse thrust, devices known as "buckets," "clamshells," or "cascades," are unlocked and moved aft behind the engines to redirect the exhaust air forward. This redirection of the air forward causes the deceleration. Reverse thrust is noisy because, just like on takeoff, the engines' power is being increased.

Slowing between 80 to 60 knots, the engines will be taken out of reverse because of the tendency they have to blow debris forward, putting it in front of the engine, where it could be ingested. Of course, reverse thrust is available to make a full stop if needed.

HIGH-SPEED TURNOFFS

In an effort to maximize the number of takeoffs and landings an airport can handle per hour, high speed turnoffs are designed as exit points from the runway. Similar to a straight off-ramp on the expressway, an airplane can turn off the runway onto a high-speed taxiway still traveling in excess of 60 knots. Runways with only 90 degree right or left turn exits require the plane to be slowed to 10 to 15 knots before the turn can be made. Spacing between landing aircraft would have to be increased because the additional time each airplane would "own" the runway.

GROUND CONTROL/RAMP CONTROL

After taxiing clear of the active runway, the ground control is contacted. Similar to taxi out, he is in charge of coordinating all the aircraft movement on the ground. At times it can seem like a long wait before receiving clearance to taxi across another active runway, or to the terminal building, but it is the ground controller's job to have the big picture and keep the flow going. There is nothing the pilot can do except wait if the taxiway leading to your gate is blocked.

Upon entering the ramp area at the larger airports, jurisdiction for ground control is transferred to the ramp controller. He is the one who knows exactly what gate each plane will be using, and if it's open. If it is occupied but the delay is a matter of minutes, the plane will probably just wait for it. If the delay is more than a few minutes, another gate will be assigned. If none of your airline's gates are open, a trip to the "penalty box" may be the order of the day. The penalty box is a specific location at an airport where you can sit and wait, without blocking any taxiways needed for the other inbound and outbound traffic.

AIRCRAFT SHUTDOWN/MAINTENANCE LOG

Parked at the gate, the engines are shut down, the seat-belt sign turned off, and a shutdown checklist completed. Any maintenance items are noted in the aircraft log book. As the pilots gather their belongings and close up their flight kits, a mechanic will call on the interphone and ask, "How's the aircraft?"

When this happens, the next flight has already begun.

AFTERWORD

Throughout this book I have emphasized how the entire airline industry is built around safety. Long before the first piece of metal is ever bolted together, the manufacturers engineer airplanes with redundant safety systems, and emergency backups for those. The airlines add the extensive preflight planning and preparation that goes into each and every flight. The pilots who are entrusted to command these air transports are thoroughly trained and tested, checked and rechecked throughout their careers. The aircraft are maintained to exact standards and inspected each flight before they are deemed airworthy. Few people outside the industry are aware of the rigorous preparations made to ensure their safety.

Pilots would like to spend more time educating the air traveler. However, an air transport pilot has very little direct interaction with his clients, the passengers. For safety and security, the FAA has mandated the cockpit door remain closed and locked during the flight. Years ago the pilots would stroll through the cabin and greet the passengers, answer your questions and ease your concerns. Today, leaving the flight deck—except for physiological needs—is prohibited. Many of those unfamiliar but quite normal noises, sounds and sensations, are left unexplained.

The pilots can talk to you on the public address system and reassure you that something like turbulence, while uncomfortable for most passengers, is nothing more than a tolerated nuisance. Unfortunately for the concerned or fearful flier, there is no time to teach. For the fascinated flier there is no opportunity to show him or her the magnitude of technical achievements.

By reading this book, I hope some of your questions and concerns were addressed. I also hope that the knowledge you acquired will edge you closer to my perspective of aviation. I still marvel at the sight of a jumbo jet flying overhead. But my fascination should not be misinterpreted as a belief that flying is miraculous. The information contained in this book should dispel that misconception.

The more you understand about flying, the more you know about the safeguards and safety checks, the more you learn about the dedication of the thousands of airline employees, the more relaxed you will feel.

I look forward to having you on board one of my flights. In the meantime, take this book along as a flight guide and "sit back, relax, and enjoy the flight."

—E.S.

AVIATION ABBREVIATIONS

A	airbus
ACM	air cycle machine
AGL	above ground level
APU	auxiliary power unit
ASA	autoland annunciator status
ATC	air traffic control
ATIS	automatic terminal information service
ATP	airline transport pilot
B	Boeing
CAT	clear air turbulence
CG	center of gravity
DH	decision height
DME	distance measuring equipment
DOT	Department of Transportation
EDC	expect departure clearance
EGT	exhaust gas temperature
EICAS	engine indicating and crew alert system
EPR	engine pressure ratio
ETA	estimated time of arrival

ETD	estimated time of departure
FAA	Federal Aviation Administration
FAR	Federal Aviation Regulations
FL	flight level
FMS	flight management system
FPM	feet per minute
g	gravity
GMT	Greenwich Mean Time
GPWS	ground proximity warning system
GS	ground speed or glide slope
Gyro	gyroscope
HMG	hydraulic motor driven generator
HSI	horizontal situation indicator
hz	hertz (cycles per second)
IAS	indicated airspeed
IFR	instrument flight rules
ILS	instrument landing system
INS	inertial navigation system
IRS	inertial reference system
KIAS	knots indicated airspeed
LAT	latitude
Lbs	pounds
LLWAS	low level windshear alert system
LONG	longitude
LOC	localizer
MCP	mode control panel (autopilot)
MD	McDonnell Douglas
MDA	minimum descent altitude
MEL	minimum equipment list
mph	miles per hour
MSL	mean sea level

N-1	engine rpm at a specific location
N-2	engine rpm at a second specific location
NM	nautical miles
NOTAM	notices to airmen
NTSB	National Transportation Safety Board
NWS	National Weather Service
OAT	outside air temperature
PCA	positive control area
PIREP	pilot report
psi	pounds per square inch
Radar	radio detection and ranging
RAT	ram air turbine
rpm	revolutions per minute
RVR	runway visual range
SAT	static air temperature
SID	standard instrument departure
SIGMET	significant meteorological information
SL	sea level
STAR	standard terminal arrival route
TACAN	UHF tactical air navigation aid
TAS	true airspeed
TAT	total air temperature
TCA	terminal control area
V-1	velocity 1 accelerate-stop speed
V-R	velocity of rotation
V-2	velocity 2 loss of engine climb speed
V-MO	velocity maximum operating (never-exceed speed)
VASI	visual approach slope indicator
VHF	very high frequency
VOR	VHF omnidirectional radio range navaid

VORTAC	combined VOR and TACAN station
VSI	vertical speed indicator
WX	weather
Z	Greenwich Mean Time (zulu time)

GLOSSARY

abeam—An aircraft is abeam a point when it is approximately 90 degrees to the right or left.

abort—To terminate a preplanned maneuver, usually referring to takeoff.

affirmative—Yes.

aileron—A movable flight control surface hinged to the trailing edge of the wing, used to control the bank (or roll) of the airplane.

AIRMET—Airman's Meteorological Information. In-flight weather advisories issued to amend the area forecast. Less severe than SIGMETS.

Air Traffic Control—Branch of Federal Aviation Administration responsible for regulating air traffic.

airspeed—The speed of the aircraft relative to the surrounding air mass. May be different than ground speed.

airway—A corridor in the sky defined by radio navigation aids.

altitude—The height above sea level (MSL), or the height above ground level (AGL).

altimeter—Pressure-sensing instrument that reads height above sea level (MSL).

angle of attack—The angle between the oncoming air and the direction of flight.

approach control—Air Traffic Control facility responsible for separation and sequencing of approaching traffic in the terminal area.

ATIS—Automatic Terminal Information Service. Continuous loop recording of the weather at an airport.

autopilot—A gyroscope-controlled device which, when "programmed" by the pilots, can keep an aircraft in a predetermined flight path.

bleed air—Air "bled" from the engines for cabin air-conditioning, pressurization, and other services.

block to block time—Time shown in airline timetables. Total time from departure to destination airport, including estimated ground time.

braking action—The slipperiness of the runway, as reported to Air Traffic Control, either by a ground crew or pilot after landing.

captain—The pilot in command. Ultimately responsible for the safety of the flight.

cardinal altitudes—Odd or even thousand-foot altitudes, from the ground up to 45,000 feet.

Category I, II, III—An ILS approach procedure and its designated minimum visibility, and decision height requirements. Typically CAT I is 200-foot AGL decision height and RVR minimum of 1800 feet. CAT II is 100-foot D.H. and 1200 foot RVR. CAT III is 50-foot alert height and 300 to 700 foot RVR.

ceiling—When more than 50 percent of the sky is obscured by clouds, the distance between the ground and the base of the clouds.

clean—Describing the aircraft with all the extendable surfaces, flaps, slats, and gear in the retracted position.

clear air turbulence (CAT)—Turbulence encountered in the air where no clouds are present.

clearance limit—The fix, point, or location beyond which further Air Traffic Control clearance is needed in order to go.

cockpit—The flight deck where the pilots fly the airplane.

compass—A directional instrument graduated in 360 degrees that aligns itself with magnetic north.

compressor—A device that increases the density of the engine intake air.

conflict alert—An automatic function of the Air Traffic Control Radar computers that warns of an existing or pending violation of minimum specified separation requirements.

co-pilot—The pilot who is next in command after the captain. Also called first officer.

crosswind—A wind not parallel with the runway direction or path of the aircraft.

decision height—The height at which a decision must be made to continue the approach or execute a go-around.

departure control—Air Traffic Control facility responsible for separation and sequencing of departing traffic in the terminal area.

dew point—The temperature at which the air will be saturated with moisture.

dihedral—The slight upward angle of the wings, designed for added stability.

distance measuring equipment—Equipment used to measure the nautical mile distance from a ground-based navigational aid.

drag—The air's resistance to moving objects.

elevator—The horizontal flight-control surface on the tail that controls the climb and descent of the plane.

expect departure clearance—When there are delays in progress on the ground, this is the expected takeoff time; also called the "wheels up" time.

expect further clearance—When there are delays in the air, such as holding, the time this delay is expected to end.

expedite—Used by Air Traffic Control when prompt compliance is required.

first officer—The co-pilot, the next in command after the captain.

final approach—The aircraft is aligned with the runway for landing.

flameout—Unintended loss of combustion in a turbine engine, resulting in a loss of power.

flaps—The movable trailing edge portion of the wing which, when extended, increases both the lift and drag of the wing.

flight deck—The cockpit.

flight engineer—The third pilot responsible for the operation of the side-facing engineer's panel. Also called the second officer.

flight level—A level of constant atmospheric pressure. Flight levels are flown above 18,000 feet in the United States.

flight plan—Specified information related to the intended flight filed with Air Traffic Control.

flight time—The actual time of the flight from takeoff to landing.

flight recorder—The general term for the "black box" usually painted a bright color. It records pertinent flight information that can be used in accident investigations.

flow control—Adjustment of traffic to ensure most effective utilization of airspace.

g force—Gravity forces that give the feeling of increased or decreased weight.

gate-hold—Procedure for holding aircraft at the gate, while waiting for takeoff sequence from Air Traffic Control.

glidepath—The electronic or visual vertical guidance beam the airplane follows when approaching to land.

go-around—Discontinuing the approach to land. Also called a **missed approach.**

Greenwich Mean Time—The time in Greenwich, England, used as the standard for Coordinated Universal Time. Standardizes time for aircraft flying across multiple local time zones.

ground speed—The speed of the aircraft relative to the surface of the earth. Will be faster or slower than the true airspeed depending on whether there is a tailwind or headwind.

handoff—The transfer of radar identification from one air traffic controller to another.

high-speed taxiway—Runway turnoff designed for exits up to 60 knots, to reduce runway occupancy time.

holding—A predetermined maneuver, usually an oval, that keeps an aircraft in a specified airspace while waiting for further clearance.

Instrument Landing System (ILS)—A precision instrument approach that gives both electronic horizontal and vertical guidance to the runway.

instrument flight rules—The procedures the pilots must follow when flying without visual cues from the ground.

international airport—An airport with Customs services available, so that nonstop service to an airport in another country can be authorized.

intersecting runways—Two or more runways that cross or meet somewhere along their length.

jet blast—High-speed wind created from the jet engine exhaust.

jet stream—Clearly defined streams of high-speed winds present at high altitudes.

knot—A speed of one nautical mile per hour, equal to 1.15 statute miles per hour, common in the United States.

landing minimums—The minimum visibility prescribed for landing while using an instrument approach.

landing roll—The distance from the point of touchdown to the point at which the aircraft can be stopped or taxied clear of the runway.

load factor—The percentage of seats filled on an airplane.

mach number—The ratio of true airspeed to the speed of sound (.82 is 82 percent of the speed of sound).

metering—A method of regulating the traffic flow into an airport, so as not to exceed the terminal area acceptance rate.

minimum descent altitude—The lowest altitude an airplane can descend on approach to land when no electronic glide slope is available.

missed approach—Discontinuing the approach to land. Also called **go-around.**

nautical mile—The unit of distance used in aerial navigation. Approximately 1.15 times a statute mile; typically used in the United States.

navaid—Navigational aid.

positive control area—Above 18,000 feet, where instrument flight rules must be followed regardless of the weather.

precipitation—All forms of water—rain, sleet, hail, and snow—that fall from the atmosphere and reach the surface.

preferred routes—Established routes between busier airports to increase Air Traffic Control system efficiency and capacity.

radar contact—Terminology used by Air Traffic Control to inform an aircraft that positive radar identification has been made.

radio altimeter—Instrument that uses the reflection of radio waves to measure height above the surface.

ramp area/apron—The defined area of the airport used for refueling, parking, maintenance, and the loading and unloading of passengers, mail, cargo.

recurrent training—Required pilot training and proficiency checks every six months.

release time—A departure time restriction used to separate traffic.

reverse thrust—The normal rearward thrust, directed forward, used to slow an aircraft after landing.

roger—I have received all of your last transmission.

rotate—To pull up the nose of the aircraft, followed shortly thereafter by the plane becoming airborne.

rudder—The vertical surface located on the tail used to control the left/right yaw of the aircraft.

runway—The defined rectangular area used for takeoff and landings.

runway visual range—Visibility along a runway measured by electronic equipment.

second officer—The flight engineer, third pilot in command after the captain and first officer (co-pilot).

short approach—A shorter than normal final approach used to expedite traffic flow and reduce delays.

sidestep maneuver—A visual maneuver accomplished by the pilot, lining up with one runway and landing on an adjacent parallel runway not more than 1200 feet to either side.

SIGMET—Significant meteorological information to warn pilots of potentially hazardous weather.

slats—High lift devices that extend from the front edge of the wing that increase both lift and drag.

speed adjustment—Adjustment in airspeed to increase spacing between aircraft.

speed brakes—Movable panels on the top portion of the wing used to slow down, increase the descent rate, or both, by increasing aerodynamic drag.

spoilers—The same movable panels as the speed brakes, which can be raised a greater degree to "dump" excessive lift from the wing after landing.

stall—Loss of lift due to an excessive angle of attack, often caused by insufficient airspeed.

standard instrument departure—A preplanned Air Traffic Control departure procedure used by aircraft to navigate from departure airport to cruise portion of the flight.

standard terminal arrival route—A preplanned Air Traffic Control arrival procedure used to navigate from cruise portion of flight to the destination airport.

straight in—The entire approach to the runway is made within 30 degrees of the runway alignment.

stratosphere—The upper atmosphere "above the weather," or troposphere.

taxi—The movement of the aircraft under its own power, on the ground.

taxiway—The designated "roadways" on which aircraft move.

terminal—A general term for an airport building used for passenger services.

terminal area—A general term describing the airspace around an airport. The terminal area encompasses apaproach and departure control.

threshold—The beginning of the runway.

touch and go—A training maneuver for practicing takeoff and landings. A landing and subsequent takeoff are made without stopping or exiting the runway.

touchdown zone—The first 3000 feet of the runway beginning at the threshold.

tower—Air Traffic Control communications facility located at an airport; usually the tallest structure with an unobstructed view of the entire airport.

traffic pattern—The prescribed airborne traffic flow at an airport, consisting of upwind, crosswind, downwind, base leg, and final approach.

trailing edge—The rear edge of the wing.

transmissometer—Electronic apparatus used to measure the runway visual range.

transponder—The airborne radar beacon used to make each aircraft's radar "blip" distinct.

turbulence—The irregular motion of the air.

vector—A change in direction issued by Air Traffic Control to provide navigational guidance.

very high frequency omni range—A navigational aid providing left and right course information.

visibility—The ability to see unlighted objects by day and prominent lighted objects at night measured in miles and/or feet.

visual approach—An Air Traffic Control approach clearance when the pilot can see either the airport or preceding landing aircraft throughout the entire approach. Radar coverage is still mandatory.

voice recorder—The "black box" that records the last 30 minutes of all cockpit communications, for use in accident investigations.

wake turbulence—General term for the disturbance of air caused by an aircraft, including wing-tip vortices.

windshear—A rapid change in the wind speed and/or direction over a short distance.

wing-tip vortices—The swirling of air behind the wing tips caused by the differential pressure on the top and bottom of the wing, with potential turbulence for aircraft following too closely.

yoke—The control column in the cockpit, used to move the flight controls and thus control the aircraft.